CW00662555

The Greatness of Dads

The Greatness of Dads

Kirsten Matthew

in association with PQ Blackwell

For my dad, Robert Harry Matthew.
And for Marc's Sofia and Tommy.

Contents

Introduction

On Sundays, I'd often go to work with my dad. It was a way for my mum, who was with me and my sister all week, to get a break, and for us to spend some time with the man who got home well after we went to bed most nights.

At his office in the city, we'd run through the quiet hallways, play on the typewriters and pocket pieces of stationery from the secretaries' desks. Dad would disappear behind his office door . . . but he was there. I'd type him notes, run down the hallway and slip them under the door.

It wasn't always easy to have a dad who worked so hard. He didn't make it to parent–teacher interviews or ballet recitals (the one time he made it to a show – an eleventh-hour arrival which meant he stood watching from the wings – I thought my heart would burst with happiness). On rare holidays away together, he'd be someone I needed to get to know all over again.

But there were and are wonderful things about my dad, Robert Harry Matthew. He gave us luxuries he didn't get as a child: a middle-class upbringing; a university education; endless encouragement. From him, I learned to question authority, to always be reading, and that, as he loves to say ad nauseam, 'Girls can do anything'. He taught me to never leave the party first, to love people for who they are, to treat friends as family, and to be loyal to the bitter end.

By the time we were teenagers, Dad had more time to be with us, and I became his confidante, his friend and, along with my sister, his pride and joy. We've danced together, travelled together and got through family crises together. We've argued and disagreed with each other. On many nights in my twenties and thirties, we sat up playing cards and

listening to music until 3 a.m. These days, we have early dinners and talk politics and books. He's beloved by my friends, the smartest person I know and still the most important man in my life.

What I've discovered from talking to fathers and children from all walks of life and from all over the world is that everyone's relationship with their dad is complicated. That's the way it should be – it's the meaning and the nature of the ties that bind us to our parents. And that's really where the motivation for this book came from. There are many books about dads already, and just as many that I couldn't or wouldn't buy my dad because the schmaltz would turn him off. I wanted to make a book that celebrates dads in a realistic, nuanced, everyday way. The result is this, *The Greatness of Dads*.

I can't claim that the idea for this book is entirely my own. It came, initially, from my friend of thirty years, Marc Ellis (see his interview on page 174). He's a dad too – to Tommy and Sofia – and this book is partly for them.

The chapters in this book follow the trajectory of our lifetimes with our dads – from birth to adulthood. They extol the things that dads do so well, and reflect on some of the things they might not (like dressing and dancing). There are pearls of wisdom from dads past and present, and some really good (and really weird) pieces of dad advice.

For the record, my dad has always been a snappy dresser and is a very good dancer, but he did, for many years, sport quite a bad combover (see left). His taste in music leans towards classic hits and country and western, and his advice is often as poetic as the lyrics of the songs he loves. I'm glad he's my dad.

Kirsten Matthew

Father

He never made a fortune, or a noise
In the world where men are seeking after fame;
But he had a healthy brood of girls and boys
Who loved the very ground on which he trod
They thought him just little short of God;
Oh you should have heard the way they said his name
– 'Father.'

Ella Wheeler Wilcox

Young Love

I'm at the age where everyone has kids, and I ask them, 'Is it like a puppy?' And they go, 'It's ten times a puppy.'

Jimmy Fallon

You don't have to be the best dad in the world; you have to be her dad. You have to be the goofy, awkward guy that everyone falls in love with. It's OK to have days where you feel like you can't hack it, or think that everyone else has it together except you; to have no idea what you're doing; to make it up as you go along.

Allison Robicelli

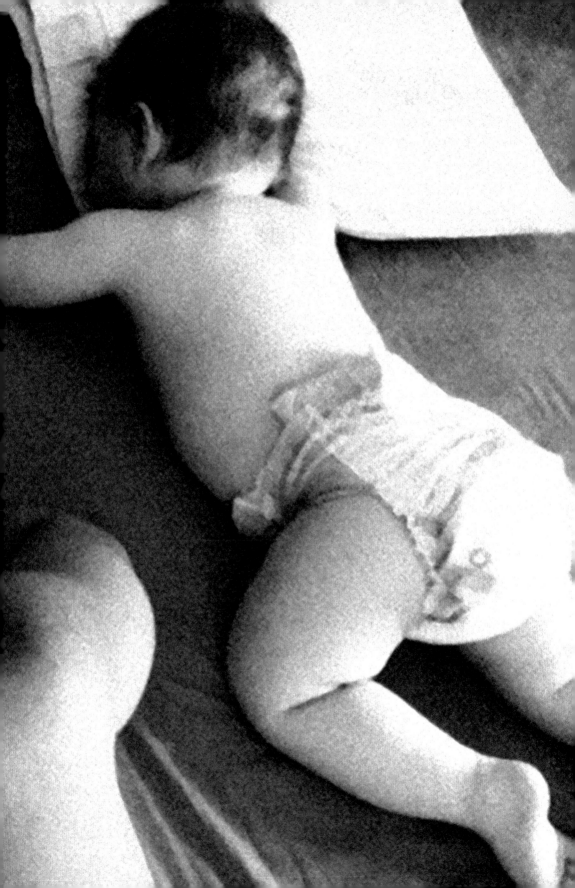

Winston Wolfe Bracewell

5, Auckland, New Zealand

My dad's name is Seth.
He works and he's a builder.
He builds high buildings.
He works all night and all day.
He doesn't do work around our house though.
He likes to go to the beach with us; watch the rugby.
I like him taking me to his buildings that he's working on, so
I can see what's happening.
He has taught me to be good. And to be nice to other people.
He taught me how to do the computer. To ride a bike. And to
wrestle.
We talk about being naughty. I get in trouble for being mean
to other people.
He says, 'Do not do it.'
He says, 'It really disappoints me.'
He is the handsomest and the strongest dad.
He's the biggest, but not the funniest.

Bearhug

Griffin calls to come and kiss him goodnight
I yell OK. Finish something I'm doing,
then something else, walk slowly round
the corner to my son's room.
He is standing arms outstretched
waiting for a bearhug. Grinning.

Why do I give my emotion an animal's name,
give it that dark squeeze of death?
This is the hug which collects
all his small bones and his warm neck against me.
The thin tough body under the pyjamas
locks to me like a magnet of blood.

How long was he standing there
like that, before I came?

Michael Ondaatje

Chloe & Lola Philippe

7, London, England

Lola: Our dad grew up in France but lives in England. On Wednesdays we go to Dad's house. And if it's Dad's weekend we stay with him. He is thirty-eight. He likes to run.
Chloe: He just did a hundred kilometres to raise money for cancer research. It took him a day and a night.
Lola: Afterwards, he couldn't walk for a day. He's a bit of a dangerous driver because he goes at full speed. It's true.
Chloe: He goes on two wheels on his side. He's crazy but safe at the same time.
Lola: He loves to play rock music. He's a pastry chef. He cooks all day at work — puddings — so it's usually Rosie that cooks for us.
Chloe: He makes our birthday cakes. He shuts the door and we can't go into the kitchen so it's a surprise. When we were six, we had a heart cake. He's taught us not to touch a steaming-hot pan. And also not to go near a fire or put the soles of our shoes by the fire. Sometimes he can be quite funny. Sometimes he tries to fix things and it doesn't work. He goes crazy when he hears thunder.
Lola: He loves chilli sauce. He puts it on nearly everything. He's wearing a pink T-shirt right now.
Chloe: Last weekend he took us to play pool and video games. We are going to France this Christmas to see our newborn cousin.
Lola: We went to Spain. We went on a tour in Brittany in our campervan.
Chloe: She dropped her ice cream on the floor and Dad wiped off the dirty stuff.

Julien Philippe

38, pastry chef, London, England

I was born in Paris. I come from a very small family. I don't have cousins, uncles or aunties – just one sister. I never had kids around me, so being a dad came as a surprise, especially when there were two of them. Their mum has a long history of twins in the family. When she was thirteen weeks' pregnant we went to the hospital and had a scan. The nurse got very flustered and asked a lot of questions and then said there were two there. It was a bit of surprise, yes, but I was over the moon about it. The first six months was like being in a dark tunnel, but, at the end of the day, you just manage.

Having twins made me understand that people are born the way they are. These girls have been together 24/7, but from day one they have had very different personalities. For me, that was a realisation that everybody is born with something inside of them - a personality. From when they were very young, that was just the way they were. Same time, same place, but completely different.

I think I'm quite a strict father - sometimes maybe too strict. I'm definitely not lenient. You have to put boundaries somewhere. I was raised that way. Your role as a dad is to be there for what you've created. We all need a father figure.

I want to be a better father to them than my dad was to me. To be present. As a child, I wasn't exposed enough to music and sports. I think it's very important because it helps you understand life a little better. Travel too – it gives them a better understanding of what's out there. We have a 1974 campervan – it's orange, and we call it *Orangina*. When we go camping, I'm happy sitting in the grass with a glass of wine. The girls are out on their bikes, making friends. It's great. The reward is when you see someone so very, very small absorbing everything like a sponge.

Their mother and I have been apart for three years now. We've had our ups and downs, but things are better now. We are on the same level with education and that's important. I live fifteen minutes' drive from their mum's home.

Obviously being a parent is not something that everyone wishes for. I understand it, in a way, from the point of view of having freedom, not being tied to anyone or having financial pressure. But, for me, the understanding of the way things work in life came from being a parent. Having kids has given me something that is invaluable. I just hope that I live up to their expectations.

He loves chilli sauce. He puts it on nearly everything.
He's wearing a pink T-shirt right now.

A baby will make love stronger, days shorter, nights longer, bankroll smaller, home happier, clothes shabbier, the past forgotten and the future worth living for.

Anonymous

It's a very rewarding experience. It's mentally cleansing. It's like washing dishes, but imagine if the dishes were your kids, so you really love the dishes.

Chris Martin

Travelling with a four-year-old boy is like transferring a serial killer between prisons.

Jim Gaffigan

The first conscious
parental thought I
ever had – cradling my
bawling three-week-
old son in my arms and
staring out the window
at the grey light crawling
over the horizon – was,
'OK. Don't kill the baby.'

Greg Knauss

I cannot think of any need
in childhood as strong
as the need for a father's
protection.

Sigmund Freud

Lawman Lynch

32, youth worker, New York City, New York, USA

My father's name was George Lynch. I assume he grew up in rural Jamaica in the parish of Trelawny — it's the same parish Usain Bolt is from. He was carjacked and murdered in 1995.

What did he do for a living? He was the quintessential hustler. His day job was working at the Jamaica post office as a postman, but he also operated a sound system called Flames Disco. He loved great music and had huge boom boxes that stood many feet tall in the air when erected. His disco was always in demand. He also had moving trucks that were available for rental, and he operated a one-man taxi service with his car. That was the job that led to his death.

He was killed when I was eleven, while I was in Mexico. I expected him to pick me up at the airport, but instead my sister's friend picked me up, which, even at that age, felt strange. Back at home, my mother called me to the room and told me. She started to cry before she could tell me, so I started to cry too. I think I was more hurt by seeing her cry than by the news. Interestingly enough, I called him twice on the day he was murdered, but never got through. The first call, he was taking a shower. The second call, he had just left the house. He died later that night.

I think his death has impacted on me both positively and negatively. My mother had had a level of dependence on my father, an expectation he didn't always live up to. After he died, I observed the strength of my sister and mother on a higher level, and they became the predominant figures in my life. But male role models are as important as female ones, and I think, as I grew older, I would have understood my father a little more and we would have come to some level of comfort as men. There are questions I wish to ask him: I want to question him about the other 'siblings' I met at his funeral. For the majority of my childhood, I knew for sure I had one sister. Then I met another. Then I met a brother. Then, at his funeral, I met about five others.

I know he was proud of me. When I passed my Common Entrance exam, an exam all Jamaican children have to take to advance to high school, Dad was very proud. The same year I was selected to represent my country at the Children's International Summer Village in Mexico, where I was when he died. He was very happy about that, and I understand why. Only the privileged in Jamaica had the opportunity to really travel. I lived in the inner city and was the child of a hard-working mother and a hustler father, and he saw this as more of an achievement for him than it was for me; he owned me and was proud of me on a different level after that.

I can't remember many conversations with my father because I was eleven when he died.

I think I saw him as someone who was always striving for success. So I live that way too: always striving for excellence.

It is much easier to become
a father than to be one.

Kent Nerburn

A man is not complete until he has seen the baby he has made.

Sammy Davis Jr

Daddy's Girl

I am not ashamed to say that no man I ever met was my father's equal, and I never loved any other man as much.

Hedy Lamarr

To be the father of growing daughters is to understand something of what Yeats evokes with his imperishable phrase 'terrible beauty'. Nothing can make one so happily exhilarated or so frightened; it's a solid lesson in the limitations of self to realise that your heart is running around inside someone else's body.

Christopher Hitchens

Una Hobday

69, retired, Bruny Island, Tasmania, Australia

I grew up in Yallourn, a State Electricity Commission of Victoria town designed for electricity workers, which had a big, open-cut coal mine. My father, George Warren Parsons, worked in the Stores section. He was just a worker — he went to work at 7:45 in the morning and came home at 4:17 p.m. every day. Mum was a teacher at the local high school.

Mum didn't meet Dad until she was thirty and he was forty-five. They met after the war. He was in the Stores section in New Guinea. She was teaching in a small town when they met; Dad was visiting his aunt in the town. They met and had a six-week romance. They fell in love in September and got married in December.

I've got a twin sister, Elizabeth. We were born when Mum was thirty, but she wasn't very well at the time so they never tried for any more children.

They were happily married for a long time and he worshipped the ground she walked on. They shared everything. We were very different from other people — their dads went off and played golf while the women did the housework. Dad helped Mum do the chores instead — he washed the floors while she did the washing — so we could all be together. He was very much a family man. They didn't have many friends or a social life. They didn't have people around for dinner. They were fairly insular in that way. We always did something on Saturdays as a family — went to the bush or for a drive. Sunday, we went to church and had a big roast for lunch.

He was a very fit man. He gardened like crazy. We had a massive vegetable garden he built on a hill. He did all the terraces, and he was always outside. Twins usually have the same warm relationship with the same parent, but I was very close to Dad and my sister to Mum. He'd talk to us all the time, explaining everything we did in the garden and telling us stories that he made up. He was interested in absolutely everything we did, and it didn't make any difference that we were girls.

He'd left school at twelve to get a job as a carpenter, but he was a great reader. He'd say, 'I'm nothing; I've got no education,' but he got four books out of the library every single week and read them all. He only liked the classics, so he didn't always approve of what I was reading, but we all read all the time. He read to us every single night. Mum, too, but I remember him most because he put on a voice for each character. They took us to every classical concert they could. And when Sir John Gielgud came to our tiny town and read bits of *Hamlet*, *King Lear* and *Romeo and Juliet*, Dad took us to see him.

We went to boarding school at thirteen. We didn't have heaps of money, but they saved and saved to send us. Dad missed us like crazy. He wrote the most fabulous letters.

As an adult, when I went nursing, he was a bit upset. He was so proud of me, but he would rather I'd been a doctor. He was the son of a doctor and his very young wife. His father went to Tumbarumba in New South Wales, where a lot of woodcutting happened, to be the only doctor in town. Dad was

only six when his dad got very ill in 1907. His mum put her husband and the kids in a horse and cart and took them to Albury and then to Melbourne to live with an aunt and their grandpa. She was just twenty-one, knee-high to a grasshopper and tough as. She travelled 300 miles with them by herself. When his father died soon after, my dad was told he was the head of the household and now responsible for the family. His mother took work as a cleaner in various houses in Melbourne. The children didn't see her very often; they were brought up by their aunt and grandfather in a lovely big house in Canterbury. But Dad always felt responsible for his mother. He wrote to her every week for the rest of her life.

As an adult, I could go and talk to Dad about anything. There was no point telling Mum stuff. Anything she wouldn't have approved of, I just didn't tell her. When my husband and I separated, I went to Dad and explained. He said 'All right, well, I'm very happy to take over the role of dad. I'll come down every weekend and do the things their dad should be doing.' Then he gave me a big hug — he was the best hugger — and said, 'Right, let's work out how to tell your mother.'

I have a son, Michael, and a daughter, Katrine. I probably wasn't as good at it as Dad, but certainly I attempted to be the kind of parent he was. When Michael was born, Dad wrote him a letter about all of the things he'd seen in his lifetime. When Michael was six weeks old, Dad watched the landing on the moon with him. The pictures were so blurry on the television, but he sat Michael on his knee and explained what a difference it was going to make in the history of the world.

Dad died when he was eighty-four, but Michael and he had an amazing relationship until then. My son could be a clone of Dad. His attitude is very much the same; the things he says. Michael met his wife when he was forty-five and married her eight weeks later. He adores the ground she walks on. He looks at her the way Dad used to look at Mum.

In our household, I'd been assigned Daddy's sidekick. Starting as a toddler, I'd kept a place standing beside him in his truck, and for the rest of his days, his lanky arm still reflexively extended itself at stop signs, as if to stop a smaller me from pitching through the windshield.

. . . Without Daddy, the wide plain of Minnesota was a vast and empty canvas, me a flealike pin dot scurrying across.

Mary Karr

Dear Malia and Sasha,

When I was a young man, I thought life was all about me — about how I'd
make my way in the world, become successful, and get the things I want. But
then the two of you came into my world with all your curiosity and mischief
and those smiles that never fail to fill my heart and light up my day. And
suddenly, all my big plans for myself didn't seem so important anymore. I
soon found that the greatest joy in my life was the joy I saw in yours. And
I realised that my own life wouldn't count for much unless I was able to
ensure that you had every opportunity for happiness and fulfilment in yours.
In the end, girls, that's why I ran for President: because of what I want
for you and for every child in this nation . . .

These are the things I want for you — to grow up in a world with no limits
on your dreams and no achievements beyond your reach, and to grow into

compassionate, committed women who will help build that world. And
I want every child to have the same chances to learn and dream and grow
and thrive that you girls have. That's why I've taken our family on this
great adventure. I am so proud of both of you. I love you more than you
can ever know. And I am grateful every day for your patience, poise, grace
and humour as we prepare to start our new life together in the White House.

Love, Dad

Barack Obama in an open letter to his daughters, Malia and Sasha,
written in 2009 prior to his inauguration

Amanda Hathaway

47, public relations executive, New York, USA

My dad, Earl B. Hathaway II, was born in Evanston, Illinois, in 1938, but grew up in Akron, Ohio. His adult life was spent in New York, Brussels, Antwerp, London and back in NYC, before he retired to Falmouth, Maine. He started his working life as a teacher before going into banking, and spent his entire career at Chase Manhattan Bank. He died in 2013.

We took so many walks together throughout my life, in various nature reserves, parks and parts of the countryside. He loved photography and capturing beautiful photos of trees, butterflies, birds and his dogs on those walks.

He took me on a tour of US colleges when I was seventeen, from New York to Boston to Chicago to Southern California — that's one of my happiest memories. When I was nineteen, I experienced a significant period of clinical depression and it turned out that he had as well. It pained us both to see the other experiencing such severe depression and we made efforts to make the other feel better, but, ultimately, we agreed that we each needed to work on ourselves for the sake of the other.

My father was an enigma. People loved and adored him, but he suffered from terrible self-doubt and -loathing.

Not until he was dying of cancer did he really recognise how much he meant to so many people. He kept everything inside and kept many secrets from his family about things like finances. He refused to talk about these things until it was too late — because he was ashamed of the financial mess he had been privately living with for so long.

On the surface, he was always impeccably dressed, wore a distinctive cologne and cooked the most delicious food. He loved classical music and philosophy. He had a huge collection of books and music. He indulged in the best cheese and wine or spirits. He spoiled his family in an effort to hide the shame, which was heartbreaking after he died because he never gave us the opportunity to help him.

In truth, he didn't live the happiest life, but he did everything he could to not let that affect the people he loved. Even though he relished solitary time, he was always warm and gracious to people when in a social environment, always asked them about themselves and made them feel welcome and treated them as special. He always found a way to laugh, even on dark days.

We took so many walks together throughout my life, in various nature reserves, parks and parts of the countryside. He loved photography and capturing beautiful photos ...

Never, never could
I expect to be so truly
beloved and important;
so always first and always
right in any man's eyes
as I am in my father's.

Jane Austen, from *Emma*

People ask me what it is like living in his shadow.
But it's not a shadow, it's cool shade.

Maryum Ali on her father, Muhammad Ali

No man can possibly know what life means, what the world means, what anything means until he has a child and loves it. And then the whole universe changes and nothing will ever again seem exactly as it seemed before.

Lafcadio Hearn

The father of a daughter is nothing
but a high-class hostage. A father
turns a stony face to his sons, berates
them, shakes his antlers, paws the
ground, snorts, runs them off into the
underbrush, but when his daughter
puts her arm over his shoulder and says,
'Daddy, I need to ask you something,'
he is a pat of butter in a hot frying pan.

Garrison Keillor

He was an excellent whistler, the kind
who can whistle through his teeth.
He drummed on the steering wheel
while he drove, and played Jim Croce's
Greatest Hits tape over and over.
If it was dark when we pulled in the
driveway, I would pretend to be asleep
so he would carry me inside.

Margaret Mason

I wanted to teach my daughter the same things I had to unlearn after years spent as a corporate lawyer: that soul is more important than money, that love means more than material things.

James Griffioen

A wedding is for daughters and fathers. The mothers all dress up, trying to look like young women. But a wedding is for a father and daughter. They stop being married to each other on that day.

Sarah Ruhl, from *Eurydice*

My mother gave me my
drive, but my father gave me
my dreams. Thanks to him,
I could see a future.

Liza Minnelli

Natalia Fedner

32, fashion designer, Los Angeles, California, USA

I emmigrated to Columbus, Ohio, from Chernivtsi, Ukraine (the former USSR), with my mother and my father, Gregory Fedner, in 1988. He was twenty-eight years old when we came to America. He's a civil engineer.

We had to leave the USSR as refugees, which meant a long journey and stays in several European countries along the way. We lived in the small seaside town of Ladispoli in Italy. I was five years old and remember being very, very scared of the sea, only going in as far as my ankles because I was convinced I would be swept away by a wave. My father, on the other hand, took great delight in disappearing beyond the horizon. He would bring me beautiful seashells from his adventures; I had a whole bag of them by the end of our three-month stay. We were poor — we couldn't take much of anything with us when we left the USSR. Any money or jewellery would have been stolen or confiscated, so the only things we could bring were tchotchkes, like decorated wooden spoons and matryoshki (nesting dolls). So we sold these at the Roman market to make money while we waited to hear about our visa status. I remember being at the market with my parents and I was never happier. It was such a pleasure.

The year I was fourteen, I spent Halloween night passing out candy with my father in Columbus, Ohio, while my mum took my five-year-old twin sisters trick-or-treating. We bought quite a lot of candy (and not just Tootsie Rolls, but the good, expensive chocolate bars). Kids started ringing the doorbell, and my dad and I took turns handing out the candy. I noticed he was giving them whole handfuls. I scolded him not to or else we would run out of candy before we ran out of trick-or-treaters. He told me that when he was a child in Ukraine they didn't have holidays like Halloween. They had tanks and soldiers that marched down the streets. He said when he saw the amount of joy in those children's eyes at getting the candy he wished he could have experienced that as a kid. So I started giving out handfuls too. And, when we ran out of candy, we ran to the local grocery store to get more.

As a teenager, there were a lot of hard conversations — too many to recollect really. My dad and I did not get along. It may sound silly now, but the hardest conversations were about my room and how messy it was. It would drive him crazy and cause all sorts of fights with my mother. For him, it didn't matter that my grades were perfect — if my room was a mess, in his eyes, I was a mess. But, for me, it was just a room. Luckily, once I moved out we were able to become friends.

His favourite place? Probably his study. It's his sanctuary away from a house full of women. He's a collector of World War II documents: bank notes, passports, journals, all sorts of SS items. He collects these items because he believes their historical significance is very important and must not be forgotten.

I think emigrating was the bravest thing Dad ever did. It took all his courage and now he is a lot more risk

I think emigrating was the bravest thing Dad ever did.
It took all his courage . . .

averse. He really appreciates the USA and how much opportunity it has given both his offspring and his mother, who immigrated a few years after us. It also puts into perspective just how bad he had it growing up in the USSR, so he is very proud to be an American and a capitalist. He mistrusts anything that borders on communism because he lived through the ravages of the system. He's never been back to the Ukraine because of how horrible it was for us and our ancestors.

My dad wanted me to have a stable job, so he was not exactly happy when I took my perfect grades to art school rather than to an Ivy League university. He had advised me to become a doctor or a lawyer, something that would give me financial security. Two art degrees later and as the owner of a successful fashion line, I'm really glad I didn't listen to him. I love that my job is my love. And my dad admitted he was wrong after Jennifer Lopez wore one of my designs. He said that he was proud of the risks I had taken and that I hadn't listened to all his warnings. I still take lots of career risks and I'm glad to know I have his approval.

When I was a youngster I lived with different families.
I nearly always felt closer to the man of the house.
Maybe because I always dreamed of having a father of my own.

Marilyn Monroe

Don't date guys who
wear gold jewellery.
It's like licking a power
switch – why would you
do it to yourself?

Sam de Brito

When it comes to men who are romantically interested in you, it's really simple. Just ignore everything they say and only pay attention to what they do.

Randy Pausch

Dear Pie . . .

```
Worry about courage
Worry about cleanliness
Worry about efficiency
Worry about horsemanship
Worry about . . .

Don't worry about popular opinion
Don't worry about dolls
Don't worry about the past
Don't worry about the future
Don't worry about growing up
Don't worry about anybody getting ahead of you
Don't worry about triumph
Don't worry about failure unless it comes through your own fault
Don't worry about mosquitoes
Don't worry about flies
Don't worry about insects in general
Don't worry aboul parents
Don't worry about boys
Don't worry about disappointments
Don't worry about pleasures
Don't worry about satisfactions
```

F. Scott Fitzgerald to his daughter, Scottie, in 1933

A Good Idea for Wintry Weather

At breakfast in the dark I pop
my dad's hat over the teapot
so that his head shall be hot
though the full buses pass his stop.

Libby Houston

Things my father taught me that stuck: How to hit the baseball off the T. All the parts under the hood of my first car. How to appreciate *The Muppet Show*. Never bring home any bikers. That I don't answer to a horn honk: that boy had better come to the door.

Sarah Brown

Garth Callaghan

46, creator of Napkin Notes, *Glen Allen, Virginia, USA*

For all intents and purposes, I'm dying. My prognosis is that I'm never going to be cured — it's really simple. I have kidney cancer.

I have one daughter, Emma. I started writing notes and putting them in her lunch when she was in kindergarten. It wasn't a thing. It wasn't a habit, for sure. They started out simply — 'Have a good day', 'I love you' — but, when Emma was in sixth grade, I was diagnosed with cancer for the first time. I started to make the notes more mature, more inspirational, more motivational. Emma started saving the notes.

If I were to be honest, I did it so that she might love me a little more than she loved her mum. I'd been the one who had gone out to work every day and I was incredibly jealous of the time my wife spent with Emma at home. When Emma was in second or third grade, my wife started working at the school. I became the de facto lunch guy.

When I was diagnosed with cancer for the third time, I read about a social movement called Because I Said I Would. It's all about making promises and keeping them. All I could think about was the implied promise to my daughter that I'd always be here. So I made a promise to write out enough notes for every day. I contacted the person behind the social movement and the local paper did a story.

Next thing my phone was ringing off the hook. In hindsight, I really wasn't prepared, but that's when publishers got in touch, movie studios, all within five days of the Napkin Notes breaking on the internet. I'm just a dad who writes on a piece of paper, and everybody can do that, but it's because I have cancer that the story resonates.

The book *Napkin Notes* was published in October 2015 in the US and has been translated into Italian, Portuguese, Korean, Japanese, Italian, Chinese and Russian. Reese Witherspoon is producing the movie. Ninety nine per cent of our lives are still normal, but one per cent is just crazy.

Having a girl gives you the best of both worlds — it's the ultimate experience in being a dad. I want Emma to grow up to be strong and confident and to look to herself for strength first. The notes are geared towards her reaching that.

We have an open, honest relationship. Any conversation that starts with 'I have cancer', is difficult. She was eleven the first time I had to explain what cancer was. However, I have never, and will never, correct her when she says, 'My dad's going to beat this.'

We're both very comfortable in our own skin and we don't really care what the outside world thinks. We both like science fiction and have sarcastic senses of humour. I'm teaching her to drive now, and spending that time with someone with a similar mindset is remarkable. We have inside jokes without even knowing we have them. We can convey volumes in five words or less. I don't have that with my wife. We just have that with each other.

My dad, Stephen Callaghan, did not communicate well and didn't know how to build up his kids. He came from

a close-knit family of Irish
Catholics and there were seven kids.
He didn't have a very good role model
for a father, but he did his best to
be a dad.

He was the local mortician in a
small town of 670 people, and I grew
up in a funeral home. I was expected
to help out in the business. Some
jobs were not cool, like washing the
hearse. I realise, as a grown-up,
that it wasn't just about the job —
it was about respect for the families
whose family member had died.

He wasn't particularly busy. He
only worked a hundred days a year, so
he was present most times. There were
times I could tell he loved being
a dad and times he was just going
through the motions. He hated going
to our high-school band concerts. He
went begrudgingly while my mum went
with enthusiasm.

He passed away before my first
cancer diagnosis, but before that,
when he'd visit us, we'd do projects
on the house together. My dad was
really good at that stuff and took
the time to teach it. He enjoyed

doing it. I don't enjoy it, and I'm
not good at it either. But I have
a lot of his old tools.

My dad was a much better grandfather than a father. When he came to
stay he would get down on the floor
with Emma or into her little princess
tent. He loved being a grandfather
and revelled in that role. As a
grandfather, you have all the time
in the world.

Post-cancer, I don't dwell on
my mortality, but I can't watch a
wedding video or think about my own
grandchildren. I can think about
today and tomorrow and next week
and next year, but when I think
about Emma as a grown-up who gets
married and has kids — well, I just
can't. If I'm lucky enough to make
it to my sixties, I hope I can sit
back and really relax and enjoy the
time I have with my daughter and my
grandkids. But the factual part of
me recognises that is not going to
happen for me. Emma says, 'My dad's
going to beat this', but do you
know what? I'm not. And that breaks
my heart.

Boys Will Be Boys

Lately all my friends are worried that they're turning into their fathers. I'm worried that I'm not.

Dan Zevin

My daddy, he was somewhere between God and John Wayne.

Hank Williams Jr

Simon Read

45, investment banker, Greenwich, Connecticut, USA

He's a mildly eccentric man, Dave Read. Born in Coventry, England, he grew up in Kings Heath, Birmingham, but he's lived most of his life in New Zealand with my mum — first in Titahi Bay, Wellington, and now in Tokoroa. He's seventy-five and retired now, but he spent his career in human resources with a large energy corporation.

He loves the Samoan culture so much he considers himself Samoan. He's fluent in Samoan; Mum is Samoan and I think he fell in love with the culture as well as Mum, so he learned the language off the bat in the early sixties. He perfected the language, and it's been said by Samoans that he knows it better than them. I believe coming from a small family and village in the Midlands had something to do with him embracing the Samoan culture of big family and the romance of a South Pacific island. He's also fluent in German, French and Spanish. He's very familiar with, but not fluent in, Fijian, Maori and Cantonese. But it's Samoa he identifies with most.

I made two seriously bad decisions in my life, and each time I knew I first had to fess up to my dad. He and Mum helped me work through them. Dad said I should never lie, and that I should be honest with myself and live life on my own terms. Eventually, that made me a stronger person and got me through. He also told me to travel in my twenties. I wasn't really going anywhere in New Zealand and was drifting along a path to who knows where. Because I didn't really apply myself at school, I was self-conscious of my qualifications and

feared being dismissed for a decent job or career. In 1995, I was offered a chance to play semi-professional rugby in Scotland and escaped. I had a sense that something greater was going to happen for me at some point. And so it was: I discovered I had a knack with people and numbers, and I found my way into a solid career in investment banking. I had one year in Edinburgh, seven in London and now nearly eleven in the USA.

My sister passed away while I was living in London. Leilani's death was an awful event in our lives; I sometimes look back and can't believe it actually happened. Dad called me on a Friday to say she was ill but was expected to be OK. I was away in Europe for the weekend and arrived home late Sunday. The phone rang and it was Dad telling me I needed to come home. I flew out of London that morning not knowing if she was alive or dead. It wasn't until I got home on Tuesday and saw the news of her death splashed over the front and back page of the local paper that I knew. Terrible.

Her death was very hard for Dad. He put on a brave face for all during that time, but he broke down with me one night after everyone had returned to normal life after the funeral. I remained in New Zealand for three months after she passed, and our big old house in Titahi Bay seemed very empty and cold, but still warm with memories. It did make things much closer between Mum, Dad and me.

Some of my best early memories are of us hiking together and him driving my sister and me to countless sporting

events around New Zealand. In 1978,
he and my mum took us travelling
around Europe for six months. It was a
legendary family trip and the memories
are still very clear for me, even
though I was only eight at the time. I
guess Dad wanted us to see his family
and Grandma again, as she was getting
on in age and he hadn't been back to
Birmingham since he left in 1957. It
was magic touring around in my late
Uncle Alan's awful pea-green Austin
Marina. We stayed in youth hostels and
met many interesting people. I had my
first cigarette outside the YHA hostel
in Koblenz, Germany — I saw some guy
toss a cigarette and I picked it
up and took a drag. It was a great
time. And for me it was an important
part of understanding how my dad's
life was created and the people who
influenced him.

I have two young boys now and
he's a wonderful grandfather, but
distance makes it tough. It's hard
living away from my parents. Leaving
New Zealand after each visit,
I wonder if this is the last time
I'll see them alive. After Leilani
died, I felt great pressure from
our extended family to return to
New Zealand. I shared those thoughts
with Mum and Dad, but they said,
'No, son, you live your life.'
Thankfully, we get home every two
years, and Skype helps. The boys are
very aware of who their granddad is
and have a loving relationship with
him. I'm guided, as a parent, by much
of what he taught me as a youngster,
but I won't be as lenient on the boys
as he was with me. Dad gave me a very
loose rein during my teenage years,
which didn't serve me well.

Dave Read

75, retired, Tokoroa, New Zealand

I was born in Coventry, England, in
1939. We were bombed out in 1940 and
moved to a ground-floor room in my
mother's brother's home with Mum, Dad
and Granddad. After some weeks, we
moved to our own rental house three
miles away, where I grew up, to age
eighteen, with my widowed mother
and younger sister. I emigrated to
New Zealand in 1957. I am still
proud to acknowledge that I came here
as an immigrant.

My wife, Loloma, and I are Simon's
parents. I was dad to a stillborn
son, Ian, in 1967, to Simon in 1970,
and to Leilani (who passed in 1999,
aged twenty-five) in 1973. I found
the hardest thing about being a dad

was striving to be consistent in
giving affection, encouragement and
punishment. And to stick to early-
laid plans to bring up our children
in the Samoan and English languages
and with some knowledge of each
parent's cultures. I was always
well intentioned, and I hope I was
loving, eccentric, ever hopeful
and never disappointing. That both
our surviving children developed
from childhood into good-looking
and nationally ranked sportspeople
was one of the most surprising and
gratifying things about being a dad.
But the most fun, the most pleasure
and joy, comes from the antics of my
two grandsons.

Of all nature's gifts
to the human race,
what is sweeter
to a father than
his children?

Marcus Tullius Cicero

My dad never grew out of his upbringing. He worked hard when he was a kid. He worked in the soil with his hands and sang gospel music, the very stuff of the American earth, and that's who he was, and he never lost that. And that stayed with me. The fact that he was such an iconic figure and praised highly by so many people, but he was not haughty and puffed up, that he was down to the earth. That mattered. Kindness. He was a kind man, he was a gentle and loving man. That's what endures. He was never angry, he was never forceful, he was always peaceful within his nature, and that's what lasts. It's what remains in the heart. A lot of people remember the darkness, or the sadness, the Man in Black. Well, there's so much more to who he was. He was asked by Larry King what he would like to most be remembered as, and he said, 'A good father'. And in that he's very successful.

John Cash on his father, Johnny Cash

When I was seven, he told everybody that, one day, I would be number one.

It actually is quite simple: My father is a man who didn't have choice in his own life. And, as a result, he wanted to give us the one thing he could: freedom for us to choose our life by giving us the American Dream. He associated choice with economics, and he wanted the fastest road to the American Dream for his kids.

Andre Agassi

I stumbled in his hob-nailed wake,
Fell sometimes on the polished sod;
Sometimes he rode me on his back
Dipping and rising to his plod.

I wanted to grow up and plough,
To close one eye, stiffen my arm.
All I ever did was follow
In his broad shadow round the farm.

Seamus Heaney, from 'Follower'

Every time I buy chips
I think of my father.

Roddy Doyle

'Why do men like me want sons?' he
wondered. 'It must be because they hope in
their poor beaten souls that these new men,
who are their blood, will do the things they
were not strong enough nor wise enough nor
brave enough to do. It is rather like another
chance at life; like a new bag of coins at a
table of luck after your fortune is gone.'

John Steinbeck, from *Cup of Gold*

I was glad my father was an eye-smiler. It meant he never gave me a fake smile because it's impossible to make your eyes twinkle if you aren't feeling twinkly yourself. A mouth-smile is different. You can fake a mouth-smile any time you want, simply by moving your lips.

Roald Dahl, from *Danny the Champion of the World*

Sherman made the terrible discovery that men make about their fathers sooner or later. For the first time he realised that the man before him was not an aging father but a boy, a boy much like himself, a boy who grew up and had a child of his own and, as best he could, out of a sense of duty and, perhaps, love, adopted a role called Being a Father so that his child would have something mythical and infinitely important: a Protector, who would keep a lid on all the chaotic and catastrophic possibilities of life.

Tom Wolfe, from *The Bonfire of the Vanities*

My father's car is marooned in a quagmire, miles up a dirt track in remote Berkshire countryside. Dad stands beside it, having abandoned the fruitless task of exhuming it from its boggy grave. He is beaming.

It is my twelfth birthday and he has contrived this adventure as a special treat for me. He has driven the family saloon as if it were an Army jeep, miles off-piste and into the mud on purpose. I am at his side, his conspirator in the mischief, and of course I am delighted.

We both know what will happen next. Dad and I will trek back to our village – it's 1964; mobile phones have yet to be invented – and call on Major Staples. The Major, who is bluff, kind and as practical as Dad is useless at anything manual, will be induced to drive out with tow rope and tool box to rescue us.

There will be a drama and that will perk Dad up no end. After we're unstuck, Dad and I will drive off – sometimes, in fact, he'll let me drive along the track, because this is the era before health and safety blighted our fun – and then go for a meal at our favourite transport café.

Charlie Mortimer

My Papa's Waltz

The whiskey on your breath
Could make a small boy dizzy;
But I hung on like death:
Such waltzing was not easy.

We romped until the pans
Slid from the kitchen shelf;
My mother's countenance
Could not unfrown itself.

The hand that held my wrist
Was battered on one knuckle;
At every step you missed
My right ear scraped a buckle.

You beat time on my head
With a palm caked hard by dirt,
Then waltzed me off to bed
Still clinging to your shirt.

Theodore Roethke

Matt Moran

46, chef & restaurateur, Sydney, Australia

My father is James Moran, but everyone calls him Jim. He grew up on a family farm in Rockley, near Bathurst, in New South Wales. There's a strong farming background in my family actually — I'm a fourth-generation farmer. Even though I live in Sydney, I was born in Tamworth, a country town in New South Wales. And I still own a working farm in the Central Tablelands with Dad. He lives at the property full-time and runs the farm, and I visit on the weekends whenever I can. We supply lamb and beef to my restaurants. He loves the farm and he's a very hard-working, salt-of-the-earth man and a great father.

From an early age, he instilled a great work ethic in me. My brother and I would get up early and help Dad on the farm, feeding cattle, mending fences, milking cows, that sort of thing. He repeatedly told us, 'Nothing comes easy, son. You have to work hard for it.' I think that's where a lot of my ambition and drive comes from.

When I was fifteen, I desperately wanted to leave school. I hated it. Trying to convince Dad that it was a good idea was tough. I told him I'd try to get an apprenticeship as a chef, but I was a bit of a troublemaker back then and he was worried that I'd drop out of my apprenticeship and wouldn't be able to get back into school. And boys from the country didn't really become chefs; they stayed on the farm. To his credit, he said he'd let me give it a go, and, looking back, that turned out to be one of the most important decisions of my life. He came around after he saw how much I loved it and how happy it made me.

Dad often tells me how proud he is of me. Whenever I update him on what's going on, he always says, 'Son, that is amazing. I'm really proud of you.' We're very close and our relationship has got even closer as we've grown older. There are idiosyncrasies that we share. Neither one of us can ever seem to sit still, and we both eat incredibly quickly — blink and the plate is clean!

The good values that he instilled in me I try to instill in my own children. They've been brought up to be honest, kind and generous, to work hard and never to be jealous of anyone. Dad loves spending time with his grandchildren and I love seeing how close he is to them. He says he feels like time spent with them is a good way to make up for the time he often didn't get to spend with me, because he was busy working the farm and earning a living for our family. He's just a good, honest, straight-up kind of bloke.

He's just a good, honest, straight-up kind of bloke.

The Railings

You came to watch me playing cricket once.
Quite a few of the fathers did.
At ease, outside the pavilion
they would while away a Saturday afternoon.
Joke with the masters, urge on
their flannelled offspring. But not you.

Fielding deep near the boundary
I saw you through the railings.
You were embarrassed when I waved
and moved out of sight down the road.
When it was my turn to bowl though
I knew you'd still be watching.

Third ball, a wicket, and three more followed.
When we came in at the end of the innings
the other dads applauded and joined us for tea.
Of course, you had gone by then. Later,
you said you'd found yourself there by accident.
Just passing. Spotted me through the railings.

★ ★ ★

Speech-days · Prize-givings · School-plays
The Twenty-first · The Wedding · The Christening
You would find yourself there by accident.
Just passing. Spotted me through the railings.

Roger McGough

Luigi Bocchino

43, portfolio manager, Rome, Italy

My father was born in a lovely town named Orvieto, which is in the central region of Umbria, just 100 kilometres north of Rome. His name is Alberto Bocchino, and he has been a surgeon for his whole life.

He lost his dad when he was three and his brother was six months old. His dad passed away in World War II, when he was thirty-six years old. It was dramatic. After the war, Italy was licking its wounds. My grandmother was quite poor and life was extremely tough for them. My father told me to 'always put your brothers first, then your parents'. I think it goes back to that time — to face life relying on each other like that built up those relationships a lot, so family is a very strict concept to him. He looks after his brother still; you wouldn't imagine that from a seventy-three-year-old.

Dad moved to Viterbo with his mum and brother when he was thirteen. He has spent the rest of his life there, apart from university, which he attended in Rome. He met my mother at university. It was unusual at that time to go to university in Italy because there were so many job opportunities — people started work as soon as possible in those days. Being a medical student was a big privilege.

My father remembers exactly the first time he saw my mum. He says that she instantly fell in love with him, but she says it's not true. The first time he went to meet my mother's father, in 1965 or '66, my grandfather told him, 'We are a serious family. If you are in, you are in forever.' My mother denies that story too, but her mother confirms it.

They have been married for forty-five years and they were together five years before they married. I have two brothers. We are all very close in age — all within three and a half years. My mum was the disciplinarian; it was her duty, the routine discipline. Dad was in charge of the extraordinary discipline. It's probably the same dynamic in my house now.

Being a father came naturally to him; he had no role model. We spent a lot of time together. My father was passionate about hunting — he would go out Saturday and Sunday, all day. I first went when I was six or seven. It's something that made us very tight and we all still like going hunting together. We hunt pheasants, rabbits and woodcock.

Every summer for fifteen years, we would travel Europe in our motorhome. Always travelling around somewhere different: Spain, France, Germany, eastern Europe. Even when I was at university, I would go away with my parents.

One brother is an orthopaedic surgeon now; the other is a lawyer. I work in finance. My father probably wanted me to be a doctor, but, when it came to make the decision, it was a tough time to be a doctor in Italy, and I wasn't ready to study day and night for ten years.

My father never really stepped into the boots of being a surgeon. He's a very good and well-known surgeon, but he's very, very humble.

You become a bit anxious about the world itself, the world your kids will live in, when you become a parent. You feel like your life has a real meaning ...

He has always dealt with people with the same helpful attitude.

He's quite a strong and peculiar character; his attitude was to always get into trouble. But he is quieter now. He has five grandchildren, including my son, Alberto, who is three, and daughter, Anna, who is one. We see him every other week. I've got a house there in the village, next to my parents' place. It was my grandparents' place and we restructured it. It's only an hour away, so we take the kids there to get some fresh air.

I became a father when I was forty; my father was twenty-nine and had much more energy for running around. But I hope to be like my dad has been to me: someone to look to as an example of consistency and honesty. I spend a lot of time with my kids, and the hardest thing is understanding when you must be kind and when to be severe. You become a bit anxious about the world itself, the world your kids will live in, when you become a parent. You feel like your life has a real meaning beyond what you always considered.

No relationship has more power than the one between a father and son. A man may be closer to his mother, have more impassioned rivalries with his brother, love his wife more desperately. But father and son – whether for good or for ill – that relationship moulds a man. A son sees in his father achievement, mastery – all the things he hopes to be. A father sees in his son potential, the possibility of all the things he has not done and may never do.

David Granger

Do I want to be a hero to my son? No. I would like to be a very real human being. That's hard enough.

Robert Downey Jr

Don't lie about stupid stuff. Don't bullshit people about places you've been or women you've slept with. You need to save your lies for really important occasions, such as salary negotiations and references for friends.

Sam de Brito

Massachusetts-based artist and graphic designer David Laferriere draws original illustrations on his son's sandwich bags every school day. He's been doing it for over eight years and has created over a thousand different illustrations. 'They love it,' he says, 'and nothing makes me happier than hearing their reaction at the end of the day.'

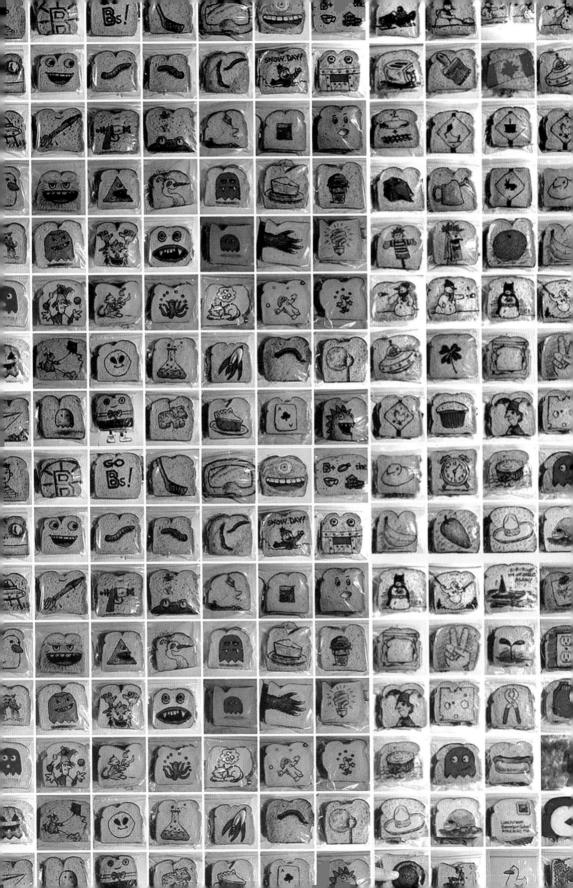

My father used to play with my brother and me in the yard.
Mother would come out and say, 'You're tearing up the grass.'
'We're not raising grass,' Dad would reply. 'We're raising boys.'

Harmon Killebrew

Every old man I see
In October-coloured weather
Seems to say to me:
'I was once your father.'

Patrick Kavanagh, from 'Memory of my Father'

'Dad?'

'Yes?'

'How big's the boat that's taking us to Portugal?'

'I don›t know really. Pretty big, I should think.'

'As big as a killer whale?'

'What? Oh yes, easily.'

'As big as a blue whale?'

'Yes, of course, as big as any kind of whale.'

'Bigger?'

'Yes, much bigger.'

'How much bigger?'

'Never you mind how much bigger. Just bigger is all I can tell you.'

There is a break, and the discussion resumes:

. . . 'Dad.'

'Yes?'

'If two tigers jumped on a blue whale, could they kill it?'

'Ah, but that couldn't happen, you see. If the whale was in the sea the tigers would drown straight away, and if the whale was . . .'

'But supposing they did jump on the whale?'

. . . 'Oh, God. Well, I suppose the tigers'd kill the whale eventually, but it'd take a long time.'

'How long would it take one tiger?'

'Even longer. Now I'm not answering any more questions about whales or tigers.'

'Dad.'

'Oh, what is it now, David?'

'If two sea-serpents . . .'

Martin Amis, from *Experience*

I hope that he will have none of my smaller and undesirable qualities and all of my better ones. I want him to grow into a man who is unplagued, regarded affectionately for his sensitivity and intelligence and candour and steadfastness and a tranquillity at the heart of his being that comes from knowing that he has been loved, that he has no obligation to carry forth a family myth, that he is unencumbered. And that he will value the company of his mother and father because he feels it is uncomplicated by our insistence that he abandon his identity for one we need him to embrace.

Alec Wilkinson

It Runs in the Family

The family, that dear octopus from whose tentacles we never quite escape, nor in our innermost hearts never quite wish to.

Dodie Smith

Aeneas carried his aged father on his back from the ruins of Troy and so do we all, whether we like it or not, perhaps even if we have never known them.

Angela Carter

Catherine Ledner

52, photographer, New Orleans, Louisiana, USA

My father, Albert, is one of the most amazing people I know. I'm biased, I know, but he really is amazing. He doesn't see things the way other people see things. He's ninety-one, a modernist architect of some renown, and is still working. He's an inventor too.

He was born in New York, but moved to Shreveport, Louisiana, as a baby. As a young child, he moved to New Orleans, where he still lives. His father sold furniture and his grandfather had the general store and post office in St. Rose, Louisiana, near New Orleans. That family was amazing; I've read things about what they did there.

Dad started doing modern architecture in New Orleans when there really wasn't a lot of modern architecture. He went to Tulane University and studied with Frank Lloyd Wright. He was inspired by Lloyd Wright, but he was very much his own architect. It's so interesting that, having grown up in New Orleans where the architecture was super Victorian, he developed the way he did, and created things and sees things so differently. He hasn't travelled or ever been to Europe.

After a while, he got a lot of recognition for his houses. He built the National Maritime Union headquarters in New York and later did two more buildings for them. One is now the Maritime Hotel in Chelsea. They are iconic because there is nothing else like them in New York.

He worked all the time when I was a child. He's still working — he's renovating a house built as a church at the moment. He had a studio that was in the back of our house. He was always home, but he was in the back working. I could bring him things, and one of my favourite memories is of making him cookies and bringing them upstairs to his studio with a cup of hot cocoa on cold days.

I was a wild child. New Orleans fit me perfectly because it's a wild kind of place. Mum was an actress when she was younger, so I remember going to plays, and my dad was very much a supporter of her and her acting. It was a very colourful upbringing, and they sent my two older brothers and me to a colourful school. Dad and Mum led by example, by how they lived their lives with goodness and kindness and integrity. In so many ways, that really had the biggest influence on me.

They let us make our own decisions. There weren't a lot of rules, particularly for me, as I was the third child. We weren't on our own, but we made a lot of decisions ourselves. They let me live my life how I wanted to and experiment in ways that many parents would have strongly objected to. They were both very open. There wasn't prejudice in our house.

I started taking pictures as a teenager, strange still-lifes. Later on, I decided that was what I wanted to do. And Dad's very proud of me — very much so.

When my son, Winston, was born I lived at home for a year. And then I rented a house a mile down the road. Later, when we'd moved to Los Angeles, Dad taught me how to step away when my son entered into young adulthood;

how not to overwhelm or pressure him. He taught me to let him make his own decisions and face whatever consequences those actions had.

Dad's a total optimist, always. Hurricane Katrina in 2005 was really hard. His house, his own creation, on the 17th Street Canal, was flooded when the canal breached. But after Katrina he came back to New Orleans and rebuilt his house. It's not exactly the same — the studio has gone — but it's very close. He saw it as an opportunity and he was one of the first to move back in after the hurricane. Then my mum passed away; that was really hard on him at the end. Now he lives there by himself and I visit about six times a year.

Interestingly, my best memories with him are being made now. I'm making a documentary about him and his designs with my cousin Roy. We've filmed in New Orleans and we'll go to film his projects in New York. I've learned a lot about him in the process and we've got to spend time together.

He was always home, but he was in the back working ... one of my favourite memories is of making him cookies and bringing them upstairs to his studio with a cup of hot cocoa on cold days.

My father had a profound influence
on me – he was a lunatic.

Spike Milligan

Geoff Blackwell
50, publisher, Auckland, New Zealand

My father, John George Blackwell, was born in 1940 and grew up in a state house on the side of Te Tatua-a-Riukiuta (Three Kings) volcano in Auckland.

He left school at fifteen after a pretty short education. I imagine he was restless to get out of school and earn his own money and become independent. He started his career in the back room of the Whitcombe & Tombs bookshop on Queen Street, before graduating to a job as a junior salesman at the publisher William Collins & Sons. My mother was working there as a secretary, and romance blossomed. They have been together ever since. Her name is Janet and she is the love of Dad's life.

Together they started their own publishing business, which had its moments but gave them a rich life together. They sold up in 1994 and have spent the last twenty two years as retired people, living a pretty good sort of life. They have been married for fifty-four years and are still madly in love. If there is truth in the statement that the best way you can love your kids is by loving their mum, then he's been a role model.

My overarching feelings for Dad are of gratitude. Our whole family adores him. He's always been wildly enthusiastic about whatever we're doing. He's hugely generous in spirit (and bank balance) towards anything that could be a positive adventure for him and Mum, but particularly for the wider family. He's always put Mum first and then the rest of us at the forefront of his life, which is quite an amazing thing. Growing up, I thought all parents were like that and I've come to appreciate just how extraordinary that is.

Our greatest adventure came when my brothers and I were at school and the fledgling family publishing business had its first major success, a book called *Men in Black*. Instead of paying off the mortgage or investing money into the business, they took us out of school and on an epic eight-month family adventure in a campervan across America, the UK and Europe. It opened up a whole new world for us, and thirty-six years and countless trips later, we still talk about it as the trip of a lifetime, one that defined our family in a way.

The boldness and 'seize the day' attitude that inspired that trip is pretty typical of the way Dad has lived his life. It has occasionally backfired, but in the big picture it has served him well.

For Dad, school was a hygiene factor. So the sooner we could get out of there the better as far as he was concerned. I was a pretty poor student and he talked me into quitting school at the end of sixth form. We went for a walk on a beach on the Coromandel Peninsula and he sold it to me in about thirty seconds flat. He said, 'Come and work for me. You can be a warehouse boy and a sales rep, and I'll get you a company car.' I said, 'You're on, mate.' I couldn't get out of school fast enough. While we had our moments working together, he taught me most of what is important in publishing, and I've always been grateful for the opportunity he gave me.

All of the good bits of me as a father come from the role model I've had, and, honestly, I think he's a pretty hard act to follow.

My brothers and I have never been wildly enthusiastic about too much advice, but it has never stopped him. He is always direct and his advice always comes from a place of generosity and honesty — if not diplomacy.

He's an uncomplicated man with a good heart. Most of his philosophy comes from the Fred Dagg playbook. Every time something good happened to our family he would break out into the chorus of 'We Don't Know How Lucky We Are'. He's a terrible singer.

Life is not complicated for Dad and I think that's been the basis for a happy life. I always joke that I don't know whether he's a genius or an idiot, because he's always been able to work out what is important

and to keep life so simple.

He's had a monumental impact on my life. He's been an amazing inspiration and example to me. All of the good bits of me as a father come from the role model I've had, and, honestly, I think he's a pretty hard act to follow. He's also a wonderful grandfather, but that's a whole other story.

We used to have some epic rumbles around the house when I was kid, but Dad has never brought a problem to my door in his whole life. I've brought a few to his.

He was my first hero and he is still my hero. I feel incredibly fortunate to be able to say that about my father.

Tell me who your father is,
and I'll tell you who you are.

Filipino proverb

As a child I didn't really comprehend my father's affection for the land . . .
My sense of injustice about our family's 'weirdness' in not owning a car was
amplified by the fact that we did not own a television either – my parents were
unapologetic about this, and told me very cheerfully that I would thank them
for it when I was older, which was quite true. But at the time Dad's refrain
'Nature looks more beautiful in the rain' was not met with good grace.
Nor was his notion that a view was something gained through effort –
scenery, for him, was something that ought to be deserved.

Eleanor Catton

I learned that work can be
meaningful from my father.
Everything he does – from his most
complex academic mathematics to
digging in the garden – he tackles
with joy and resolve and enthusiasm.
My earliest memories of my father
are of seeing him work at his desk
and realising that he was happy.
I did not know it then, but that was
one of the most precious gifts a
father can give his child.

Malcolm Gladwell

Fabio De Bernardi

36, account director, London, England

My father, Luciano De Bernardi, was born and always lived in Busto Arsizio, just outside Milan, Italy. It's where I and my two elder siblings were also born.

He was a salesman in the old-school way, a bit like Arthur Miller's *Death of a Salesman*, smashing tens of thousands of miles on the road each year with his samples of wood flooring and carpet in the car's boot. I'm in sales myself now, but it doesn't sound anywhere near as heroic and grinding as his type of selling was. And, funnily enough, what he always told me when I was in school was, 'Do everything you want in life, but don't be a salesman . . . it's an ungrateful job.' The irony of it.

My mum died of cancer in 1988. I still remember that day. He came home from the hospital, grouped us in our bedroom and told us that Mum was dead. I was only eight years old and I didn't really understand most of what was going on, but that image will always be with me.

After that, when my father was on the road working, my sister, who is almost twelve years older than me, took on the role of mother to me, and, to a lesser extent, my brother (who's seven years older than me).

My dad always had a passion for motorsports, which my brother and I followed. In his spare time, he volunteered as one of the race stewards. Some of my best memories of him are when we went together to Monza racetrack outside Milan. He also always loved trains, both models and real ones. He travelled quite a bit in Italy and Europe to see certain historic trains, with a group of friends or even on his own sometimes. When he retired, I worried that he may quickly get bored, but instead he started going to see even more trains and made the best of his leisure time.

I think he was OK being on his own after Mum died. In the end, it made him a bit of a lone wolf. He attempted a relationship with a much younger woman a few years after my mother's death, but that didn't last very long at all. Maybe that was an attempt to move forward. In the end, I think that the love and satisfaction my siblings and I gave my father was very important to him and he was happy and content with seeing that his children were all doing fine in their respective lives. And by fine I don't mean rich or powerful, because those were not the things he cared about or the values he brought us up with.

I moved to London nine years ago. I had always lived at home with Dad before leaving for London. I felt like his life companion, in a way. However, when I was twenty-seven, I decided that I was going to London to start my own web company. When I asked him how he felt about it, worrying that he may have felt abandoned, he smiled and told me to 'go and follow my path', since he'd not done it himself when he was younger and he regretted not having made the choices he wanted to make.

He was killed by a stroke a few months later, at the age of sixty-eight. That happened just a few days before he was supposed to come and visit me in London for the first

It's definitely true that men become like their fathers.
I have his kindness, curious mind . . .

time. I was really looking forward to showing and sharing with him my new life — where I lived, worked and all that.

It's definitely true that men become like their fathers. I have his kindness, curious mind, humour and strength in the face of adverse luck. But I also have his worrying, mood swings and a tendency to isolate myself if things don't go as I want them to. With all due respect to my father, I'm determined to smooth out some of those attributes. I started psychotherapy three years ago. I now know myself a lot better and I understand my father a lot better — the way he was and the way he acted. I believe he struggled with being in touch with his own feelings. He was a loving, caring father and I have the fondest memories of him, but I think that he struggled with the rigid, fascist upbringing he received.

My grandfather was born in 1903 and was a supporter of Mussolini and fascism. Emotional intelligence definitely wasn't a top subject for discussion.

My father couldn't tolerate chaos — loads of people, noise, bad manners. His favourite places were Switzerland, Austria and Germany, mainly because he saw them as places where discipline and order were taken seriously (as much as he, and his own father before him, took them seriously).

When I dream of my dad now, most times I am hugging him and not vice versa, as if I am letting him know that everything will be all right, whatever happens. It's funny, because, in my memories of him, it is him who would put an arm across my shoulder, in what was his way, to give you a cuddle. There he is, this six-foot-four man, very often wearing a serious face, with lips pursed and bright eyes, giving warmth and love.

Dads are stone skimmers, mud wallowers, water wallopers, ceiling swoopers, shoulder gallopers, upsy-downsy, over-and-through, round-and-about whoosers. Dads are smugglers and secret sharers.

Helen Thomson

I never really knew my own father. I was raised by a single mom and two wonderful grandparents who made incredible sacrifices for me . . . But I still wish that I had a dad who was not only around, but involved; another role model . . .

That's why I try to be every day for Michelle and my girls; what my father was not for my mother and me.

Barack Obama, on celebrating Father's Day weekend

in his weekly address from the White House, 2015

Lovely walk this morning with Father, who grows old with a very graceful philosophy. Comparing bees and butterflies to elephants & parrots & speaking of indentures with the leveller. Barging through the hedges and over the walls with the help of my shoulder, blaspheming and stopping to rest under colour of admiring the view. I'll never have anyone like him.

Samuel Beckett, to a friend, 1933

Stefano Vegliani

56, sports reporter, Milan, Italy

My father, Franco Vegliani, was a prisoner of the British Army for four years in North Africa. He went into the army because it was compulsory. He wasn't just a soldier; he was an officer. He was sent to northern Africa because of his knowledge of German. After the Battle of El Alamein, he and a general were in a car escaping from the battle and they ran out of gasoline. Far away, they saw cars and tanks, and they thought they were Italians or Germans. But they were British and they got them as prisoners.

Being a prisoner of the British Army in World War II wasn't like being a prisoner of the German army. There were a lot of Italians and they built good friendships in there.

His retelling to me and my younger brother was so rich that I could imagine the camp with big tents. It was as though life there ran like a small village. No one had to do any real job; they just had to spend the time. It was quite comfortable. They didn't have freedom to go anywhere, but the weather was good and it wasn't difficult to live. He wanted to be a writer, so he spent a lot of time writing and reading and had a lot of time for himself. He was freed in 1946, one year after the war ended, and he always had good feelings about the British; he never blamed them.

After the war, he lived his life in Milan, but he was born in Trieste, a very special, old land that was part of the Venetian Empire. He grew up in Fiume, which is now Rijeka, Croatia. He went to Bologna for university. Fiume was once Yugoslavia, but when he was there, and until the war, the territory was Italian. He went to Milano because his parents had escaped from Fiume when there was a big exodus of Italians.

He wanted to be a writer, not a journalist, but it was difficult to live, to have a salary as a writer, so he became a journalist. He worked for a weekly magazine, *Tempo*, which was something compared to *Life* magazine. He told funny stories about that time, about going to Monte Carlo with a photographer, looking for Maria Callas, who was there with Onassis; about meeting kings around Europe. Because he could speak German, he went to San Diego in 1967, for *Tempo*, to meet Herbert Marcuse, the philosopher. While he was flying to America, Robert Kennedy was killed, so he followed the story for the magazine.

In the second part of his career, he went into economics reporting. He moved from *Tempo* to a monthly magazine that was focused on economics, and he wrote about the big industrial families of Italy.

He was a journalist with 'a good pen' — he had a style. He wrote a few books, but he really didn't have the success that he could have had. A few of his books were republished after his death, and one novel, *La Frontiera*, became a film in 1996. It's about a soldier who goes home from World War II and meets someone who tells him stories about World War I. Probably some parts of it relate to stories that he heard when he was young. All writers put something of themselves in their books.

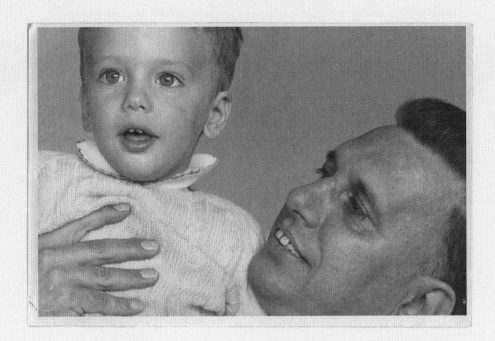

He was a great reader. He loved philosophy, was passionate about Marcuse. He would read books by writers from Trieste, in Trieste dialect. In the evening — it was nice — he would tell these stories to my mother and me and my brother. He would tell his own great stories of fantasy and real life too. He would tell very funny stories about being a prisoner.

When I was eighteen, I wanted to be a photographer. I did some jobs with my father — him writing and me taking pictures. But then I collaborated with a magazine on sailing and I started writing. That was the beginning of my career in journalism. I am different to him — I don't have 'a good pen' — so I chose to be a TV journalist. I like to work with video because it uses the image. He really didn't care about me being a journalist. He never pushed me; he left me to be free to do what I want. My father didn't have too many rules; that was mostly my mother. It's not always like that — there are fathers who are very severe in Italy.

He died in 1982, at the age of sixty-seven. When he came back from North Africa and the prison camp, he contracted TB, and later he had heart disease. He died of a heart attack. He was still writing for himself and for a few magazines. So many times, after he died, I would think, 'I wish my father was here.' When I really needed to have his help, he wasn't with me.

He was already dead when I became a father. My son, Simeone, is fourteen years old now. He was born in Trieste, like my father, and we go a few times a year. We have cousins there. My son loves to listen to stories about my dad. I am not so able to tell stories of fantasy like my father, but because they were born in the same place and he can see his books, there is something magic in that person for him.

One of the greatest gifts my father gave me –
unintentionally – was witnessing the courage with
which he bore adversity. We had a bit of a rollercoaster
life with some really challenging financial periods.
He was always unshaken, completely tranquil, the
same ebullient, laughing, jovial man.

Ben Okri

Parents rarely let go of their children, so children let go of them. They move on. They move away. The moments that used to define them – a mother's approval, a father's nod – are covered by moments of their own accomplishments. It is not until much later, as the skin sags and the heart weakens, that children understand; their stories, and all their accomplishments, sit atop the stories of their mothers and fathers, stones upon stones, beneath the waters of their lives.

Mitch Albom, from *The Five People You Meet in Heaven*

I came back from university thinking I knew all about politics and racism, not knowing my dad had been one of the youngest-serving Labour councillors in the town and had refused to work in South Africa years ago because of the situation there. And he's never mentioned it you just find out. That's a real man to me. A sleeping lion.

Johnny Vegas

My father was my inspiration. He taught me that nothing comes without hard work, and demonstrated to me what hard work meant as a shift worker with two jobs. He taught me to be passionate about fairness. He taught me to believe in Labor and in trade unionism. But, above all, he taught me to love learning and to understand its power to change lives.

Julia Gillard

Mayra Armstrong

41, real estate manager, Apex, North Carolina, USA

My dad, Dr Jose Alejo Garza, was born and raised in Monterrey, Mexico. He is a character and has some very funny stories about growing up in Mexico. He'll tell you how he used to eat weird things, anything that could fit in a pot, including toads, at his dad's ranch. They didn't have a lot of money — as a kid, when he'd give a present at a birthday party, he'd only be able to give a tube of toothpaste or a bar of soap. He didn't get to travel with his family.

He came to the USA after he finished medical school in 1973 with a dictionary because he didn't speak proper English. He went to school, worked hard, did a year in the air force. He gets offended when people talk about the wetbacks in Mexico, because he worked hard. He says he did it the right way, and he's proud of everything he's accomplished.

He was a very good doctor, but he's seventy-one and retired now. He did open-heart and brain surgery anaesthesia. My mother and him got together in Mexico. They have been married for forty-one years and live in San Antonio, Texas.

Ours was a very traditional childhood. My dad was very strict, Mexican macho style. I have two sisters and one brother and we had to follow the rules. Everything had to be clean and in its place — no feet on the sofa, no handprints on sliding doors. We had to do chores, earn our money. We had to come home on time; we had to finish university or we couldn't live under his roof; and there were no tattoos or piercings allowed. They were just the rules. I was the black sheep and got in trouble the most; I guess I was the rebel in the family.

I can't say it was perfect, with no ups and downs, but we had horses, dogs and ducks. We lived on two and a half acres, with stables, and we took riding lessons because my dad loves horses. We each got a car on our sixteenth birthdays. I went to Europe for two months for my quinceañera.

He always told me to marry someone at least six years older than me; I don't know why. But my husband is six years older than me. I met him when I went to visit my uncle in Hong Kong. We have two kids: Alec, who is eight, and Milla, who is six.

I think it's thanks to my father's hard work and strict rules that I am a good parent today. My children

He's very spontaneous. He's capsized boats; he got his licence to fly a plane. He told my mum he was going for coffee once and came back with a motorcycle and a Maserati . . .

knew from an early age how important it is to study and that they are expected to go to university. I think it is very important to set rules and to be respectful, to not talk back, to come home when you are supposed to. My husband, John, is a lot more relaxed.

Dad is a lot more relaxed now too. My mum has taught him to enjoy things. He's very spontaneous. He's capsized boats; he got his licence to fly a plane. He told my mum he was going for coffee once and came back with a motorcycle and a Maserati. Until a few years ago, he would waterski on one ski. I am surprised he still has all of his fingers and toes. He keeps busy with numerous hobbies — fishing, travelling — and was flying his plane until last year. And he is a fantastic grandparent. He visits us often and does so many things for the kids. My mother has told me that he does things for my kids that he never did for us — changing diapers, helping with baths — because he was always working. Now he reads the news from Mexico on his iPad every morning when he has his coffee, helps around the house and is a very happy grandfather.

I thought my father, who
hated guns and had never been
to any wars, was the bravest
man who ever lived.

Harper Lee, from *To Kill a Mockingbird*

Driving down a nice two-lane highway, summer day, Ann Arbor, Michigan.
I'm in the backseat of a '49 Cadillac. Always had a good car, my dad.
Frank Sinatra's singing: 'Fairy tales can come true / It can happen to you /
If you're young at heart.' My dad's singing along. From that moment on,
when people asked me what I wanted to be, I would say, 'A singer'.

Iggy Pop

Dressed to the Nines

Every dad is entitled to one hideous shirt and one horrible sweater. It's part of the dad code.

Tom Baker in *Cheaper By the Dozen 2*

He was dressed in his standard around-the-house outfit, which is to say, his underpants. No matter the season, he wore them without a shirt or socks, the way a toddler might pad about in a diaper. For as long as any of us could remember, this was the way it went: he returned home from work and stepped out of his slacks, sighing with relief, as if they were oppressive, like high heels. All said, my father looked good in his underpants, better than the guys in the Penney's catalogue, who were, in my opinion, consistently weak in the leg department. Silhouetted in the doorway, he resembled a wrestler.

David Sedaris, 'Laugh, Kookaburra'

If I can walk around in my underwear and pull them up super high so that it's just gross looking and then try to be very serious with them, I like to do that . . .

Paul Rudd

There wasn't a mirror my father could pass by without looking in it. He would stand next to me and look in the mirror and say: 'I'm still handsome; you get your looks from me.'

Maryum Ali on her father, Muhammad Ali

Sally Steele

44, fashion stylist, Brisbane, Australia

Although small of stature, Dad was a giant to me. He was a hero, an action man, and as a kid I wondered at his gymnastic ability, boundless energy and his love of adventure.

His name was Andrew Ramsay McLeod Cunningham, but everyone called him Ramsay or Rams. He grew up on the south side of Glasgow, Scotland, in a wealthy suburb called Whitecraigs. He went to a private school and Glasgow university, where he was the gymnastics and judo champion.

His degree was in mechanical engineering, but he could do pretty much anything. He built cars, rebuilt houses, was a pioneer in the frozen-food business in the late sixties and early seventies. Then he saw an opportunity in the Middle East for refrigeration engineering and air conditioning. Eventually he moved into project management for big projects like hospitals, airports, military cities, palaces, causeways and Euro Disney. In his spare time he built golf courses in the desert.

He spent most of my life abroad, working in Saudi Arabia, Yemen, Bahrain, Pakistan and Paris. My brother and I were given the option to go to boarding school or stay at the schools we were at and live part of the year with grandparents and family friends. My mother lived with Dad for three or four months and then spent three or four months back in Scotland with us.

I spent all my school holidays with them, wherever they were. In Pakistan, Dad was heading up a new international airport and we lived in a gigantic, empty marble mansion. We had security guards patrolling the streets with Kalashnikovs because of the bandits. We had ten or twelve servants who did everything for us, mainly because my dad couldn't say no to people who needed to support their families. He was very kind and good, and generous to a fault to everyone he interacted with. He used to say, 'No one ever got poor from giving.'

As a young kid, just being in Dad's company was enough — I loved just hanging out with him. Everything was an adventure, and even if we broke down from no petrol he would freewheel the car and make out he had done it on purpose. Dad didn't see anything as a problem.

Our relationship suffered during my teens. When I was eighteen, I told him that after all his years overseas he didn't know me at all, and that if he didn't try to get to know me as an adult then we would have the same relationship he had had with his father. It resulted in a huge argument and us falling out for a few months, until he surprised me and came to the Paris restaurant where I was working and sat down at a table.

When I was twenty, at the University of St Andrews, he surprised me while on a business trip to London by bringing me an Alfa Romeo, as my car had broken down. We hung out together, just the two of us, for the first time since childhood. He met my lecturers, my friends and flatmates, came to my local coffee shop. We watched a friend in *Macbeth* in the cathedral ruins, under the stars, drinking whiskey from a hip flask to keep away the chill. Afterwards, he treated my friends and

me to dinner at a local curry house and regaled the collected company and waiters till closing time with his desert adventures. I glowed. From then on, we had a wonderfully close relationship until he died in 2013.

Dad was a feminist in that he believed I could achieve anything I put my mind to. He showed me how to check a car for rust and other major issues, change a tyre, clean spark plugs. He told me to always carry a pair of tights in case I had to repair a fan belt, which I did in 1990 in the countryside between Andorra and France. He advised me to say yes to every opportunity that comes my way, and work out how to do it afterwards.

Despite his affinity for always looking well put-together, he actually had no dress sense. He had his own personal stylist — my mother — and had only to put on the pressed clothes laid out daily on his bed. When left to his own devices, it was a lottery — he could easily turn up covered in oil, clashing colours, old, ripped rugby shorts, long socks, Swedish clogs and a fur trapper's

hat, caring not a jot. So, I think I got my adventurous and daring style sensibility from him. He would always say how amazing the pieces I put together looked. He always encouraged me to push the boat out more. I remember going out to a club at sixteen wearing my brother's old navy hat and uniform with a rah-rah skirt and Dr Martens. While he was saying how fantastic I looked, all the other parents at the dinner party they were hosting were kind of shocked. I loved that about him, and really make sure I let my daughters express themselves in their clothes now.

When he retired, my brother and I sponsored my folks to emigrate to Australia, and they lived here until he died. One of the biggest things I miss is that he was always interested in and enthusiastic to hear about my work ventures, ideas, projects and dreams. In his final years, he would pop in for a coffee on the way back from a doctor's visit or errands and just listen. He'd never give advice, but always say how great what I was doing was. No one else is that person in my life now.

I remember opening my dad's closet and there were, like, forty suits, every colour of the rainbow, plaid and winter and summer. He had two jewellery boxes full of watches and lighters and cuff links. And just . . . he was that guy.

Jon Hamm

Dad was six foot two and long-legged, taller and stronger and with a more beautiful voice than anybody. His hair was salt-and-pepper; he had the broken nose of a boxer and a dramatic air about him. I don't remember ever seeing him run; rather, he ambled, or took long, fast strides. He walked loose-limbed and swaybacked, like an American, but dressed like an English gentleman: corduroy trousers, crisp shirts, knotted silk ties, jackets with suede elbows, tweed caps, fine custom-made leather shoes, and pyjamas from Sulka with his initials on the pocket. He smelled of fresh tobacco and Guerlain's lime cologne . . . Not only women but men of all ages fell in love with my father, with that strange loyalty and forbearance men reserve for one another. They were drawn to his wisdom, his humour, his magnanimous power; they considered him a lion, a leader, the pirate they wished they had the audacity to be.

Anjelica Huston on her father, John Huston

My Father's Hats

Sunday mornings I would reach
high into his dark closet while standing
on a chair and tiptoeing reach
higher, touching, sometimes fumbling
the soft crowns and imagine
I was in a forest, wind hymning
through pines, where the musky scent
of rain clinging to damp earth was
his scent I loved, lingering on
bands, leather, and on the inner silk
crowns where I would smell his
hair and almost think I was being
held, or climbing a tree, touching
the yellow fruit, leaves whose scent
was that of a clove in the godsome
air, as now, thinking of his fabulous
sleep, I stand on this canyon floor
and watch light slowly close
on water I'm not sure is there.

Mark Irwin

Katie Ferrara

27, musician, Los Angeles, California, USA

My dad, Ronald Bruce Ferrara, grew up in Metuchen, New Jersey, but he lived his adult life in Pennsylvania, Italy, San Francisco and Los Angeles. He had different temporary jobs when I was growing up, and there were periods of time when he didn't work because he was recovering from chemotherapy. He died ten years ago, so the best memories I have of him are of when I was young girl and he used to read to me every night and we'd go on nature walks together on the weekends.

My dad listened to jazz and music from the 1940s and his favourite radio station was National Public Radio. He always wore a red cotton beret and a clip-on solar shield on his eyeglasses. He loved Dante's 'Inferno' and *Cinema Paradiso*, and his favourite place to be was in the backyard of our house.

He was a spiritual man who didn't need a lot of material things to be happy. He was a fighter and always told me he was going to live until 100. He never got mad or emotional; he had a calm demeanour and always smiled, and he never let his cancer affect his positive outlook on life, even at the end.

His best advice? Always forgive others, even if they hurt you badly. I wish he was around to give me more advice.

The hardest conversation I had with my dad was about the possibility of him dying. He brought it up when he was driving me home from a rehearsal. If he had anything difficult to discuss with me, he would always do it when he was driving me somewhere. Perhaps it was because we would both have to face the problem without the opportunity of running away.

When I was about twelve and first started wearing lipstick, my dad would ask, 'Are you wearing make-up?' I would say back, 'You're wearing more make-up there than I am!'

Georgia May Jagger on her father, Mick Jagger

A turtleneck is the most flattering thing a man can wear . . . because it establishes the very standard for flattery in fashion, which is that nothing you wear should ever hide what you want to reveal, or reveal what you want to hide. This is the certainty from which all the other certainties proceed; this is why my father, never a religious man – indeed, a true and irrepressible pagan, literal in his worship of the sun – believes in turtlenecks more than he believes in God.

Tom Junod, from 'My Father's Fashion Tips'

The week before we set off, the girls (Edie, thirteen, Georgia, eleven) gave me a list of things I wasn't allowed to wear, at least not while I was in their company. This was quite a litany and included flip-flops (unmanly, apparently), 'man jewellery' (gold watches, neck chains, earrings or 'gay' bracelets), training shoes (they listed these twice), cycling shorts (although why anyone would want to wear cycling shorts on a beach holiday is beyond even me) and anything yellow, orange or 'hot pink' (fair enough).

Having been given this list, I made the mistake of asking if there were other things I shouldn't wear or do, and was rewarded with a barrage of items that led me to believe they'd been thinking about this for some considerable time.

Dylan Jones

Marc Ellis

44, sportsperson and entrepreneur, Auckland, New Zealand

I am an only child, so for me, as a kid, my dad was part Superman, part soothsayer and 100 per cent my best friend.

Chris Ellis was born in July 1942 in New Zealand. He lived in Melbourne till about age seven, I think, and then lived in Wellington, where my parents raised me. He had an upbringing in a more traditional time, when there wasn't a lot of emotion shown. His father would come home, eat dinner alone. They'd give him a kiss on the cheek before going to bed and that was as much as they got emotionally. He was able to sit back and witness what he didn't have growing up and then make sure he gave it to me.

His father never came and watched him play sport, but Dad didn't miss any of my games. Every Saturday, we'd go and get out of the house while Mum had a sleep in. We'd go boot a ball around for two or three hours at the park and get a Sparkling Duet on the way back from the shops.

He had a huge amount of energy then. I had my kids ten years later in life than he did and I'm not sure I have the energy he had. There were probably times he didn't want to get off the couch, but he always did.

That's part of the challenge of having an only child, I guess. I remember him making me a trolley because I loved trolleying. One day, despite having no practical abilities, he spent hours adding a back axle with some springs on it. He cut his hands to bits. I'll never forget him doing that, because it didn't come naturally.

My old man's always had a healthy disrespect for authority. He's principled. And he's a peacock — his dress sense veers on the side of costume. When he'd come to my school rugby games, he'd dress like he'd just come off the ski slopes in a one-piece red après-ski suit with a crocheted woollen hat and matching red moonboots. He had never skied a day in his life! It was my first taste of playing sport under extreme pressure.

There were photos on the wall at home when I was a kid of him in his Speedos, in a pose with the heading 'Mr Wellington 1982', which was funny when I was eight but pretty awkward when I was fourteen, and girls would come around and say, 'Why's your dad such a dick?' But I think it reflects his joy for life, his enthusiasm and humour.

He gave me two bits of writing at two important stages of my life. There was 'Desiderata' (see page 276) when I started university. He said, 'Live your life by this and it will be a good life.' Still to this day, I pick it up and read it. 'If' (see page 265) by Kipling he gave me when I was in my early thirties. But his best advice was, 'If it feels good and it doesn't hurt anyone, do it.'

I don't think there's been a time when he's been most proud of me. That's the cool, consistent thing about it. The worse it gets, the more he's got my back. And it's unconditional. That's the uniqueness of the bond between parent and child. If you have a dad who gives you that security of knowing there's someone in your corner, that's pretty unique.

One day soon, though, that will go. He and my mum have been living in Auckland, where I live, for ten years. Dad and I catch up for lunches; he likes a cold beer and a couple of oysters. We'll grab lunch together, talk about business, family. But he won't be in my corner forever. Recently he said, 'I'm starting to feel my age because all my mates are dying.' That must be a pretty ordinary situation.

By the time they get to a certain age, they've seen it all. I'm thankful for what my parents have given me, and while I'm not an overtly religious person I say a prayer every night, part of which is for me to look after them as they've looked after me. The tables do turn and you hope you can repay their kindness for many, many years, with patience and time.

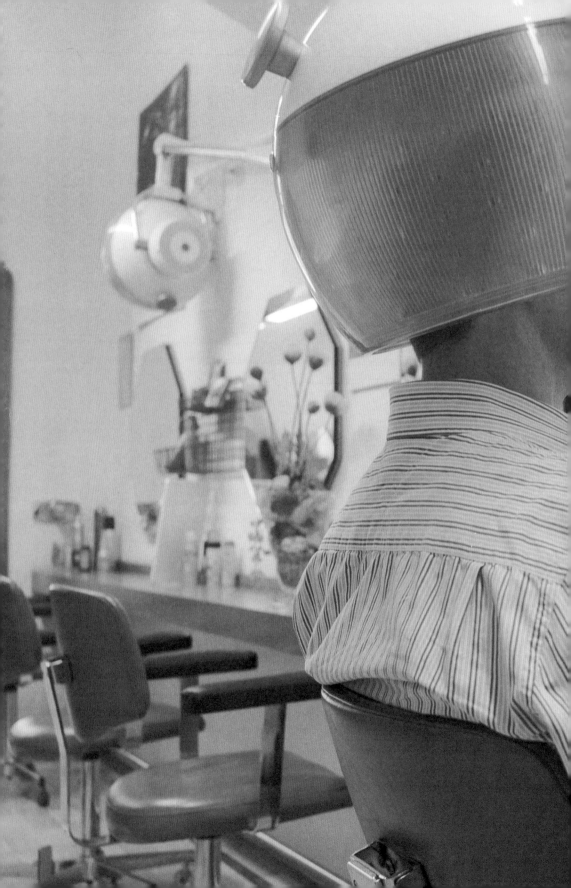

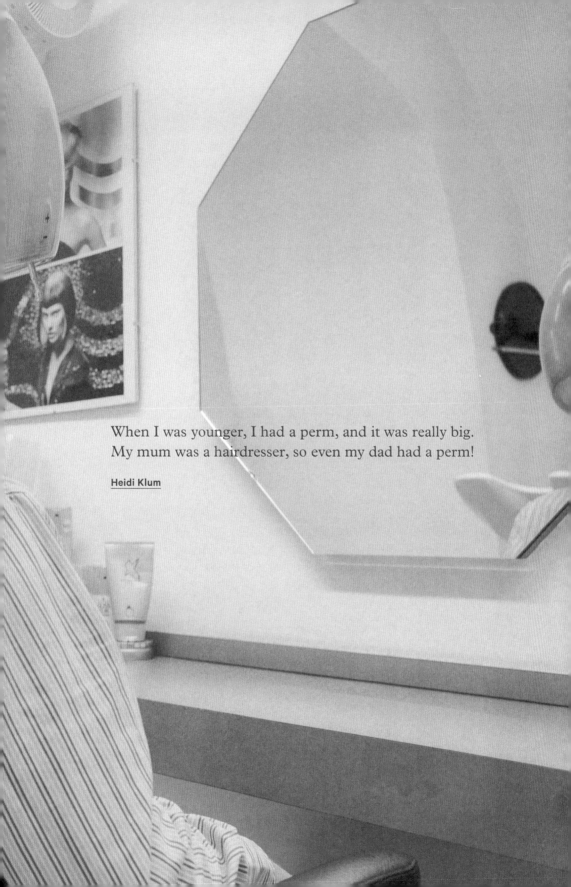

When I was younger, I had a perm, and it was really big. My mum was a hairdresser, so even my dad had a perm!

Heidi Klum

Few men in their seventies
looked as good as my father did.
What was his secret? Genes,
maybe, since he didn't exercise
or diet, and he kept a candy
drawer, drank a pot of black
coffee every day, and read in
the middle of the night. Still, he
took such joy in being a dad –
and in life in general – and his
happiness showed.

Jennifer Grant on her father, Cary Grant

The only advantage to being a middle-aged man is that when you put on a jacket and tie, you're the Scary Dad. Never mind that no one has had an actually scary dad since 1966. The visceral fear remains.

P. J. O'Rourke

Angela Morgan

43, event manager, Auckland, New Zealand

My dad, Norman Francis Morgan, grew up in Nairobi, the capital and largest city of Kenya, on a farm. He was the youngest of five — three brothers and two sisters. When he was around twelve, he and some of the family travelled by boat to Australia, where they resided in St Kilda, Melbourne. When he was fifteen, he moved to New Zealand, with his parents and one brother, where he remained, in Lower Hutt, Wellington.

When he first arrived in New Zealand, he started working as a printing apprentice and he remained with the same company for over thirty years. After he was made redundant, he moved into an IT and administration role, until he passed away suddenly three years ago on 26 September at the young age of sixty.

I remember him for his curries, his love of punk music, The Shadows, Freddy Fender, his harmonica and guitar. And his terrible black short shorts — he had these short shorts that would put Britney Spears to shame! Mum even threw them out once and bought him new ones, and good old Dad went to the bin and grabbed the old ones out.

Being an only child and getting 100 per cent attention from your mother and father can be quite full on, but it also means you are always being looked out for by one or the other. Dad was particularly protective, which I think came down to the fact that I was his little girl. When I was around seven, there was a ten-year-old who lived a few houses up from us on the same side of the street. He was an oversized boy with a big head and squinty eyes and had a mouth trashier than Lindsay Lohan — he was such a bully. He used to try to run me off the street on his bike if I was riding mine. He'd throw things at me and tell me the usual things horrid kids do — 'You're ugly' or 'You're fat', et cetera. One day I was playing at the local playground and he and his snotty-nosed little brother cornered me and said if I didn't get out of the playground they would beat me up. I started running to get my bike and, as I was running, I felt a thud in the middle of my back. One of the boys had thrown a rock at me. I sprinted to my bike and pedalled as fast as I could back home. I told Dad what had happened, and holy hell was he mad. He spent the next few minutes cooling my welt with a cold cloth, talking to me in those soothing dad tones, saying, 'Don't cry, Bubby' (my nickname). Then he put me in our family wagon and we drove to the playground. I can remember the kid's face to this day as my six-foot-one dad walked up to him, me trailing behind, saying, 'Come here, boy!' If this happened today, my father most likely would have been arrested, but he grabbed the boy by the shirt front, made him apologise to me and promise to never do anything like that again. We drove home in silence, and once we got there he patted me on the head and said, 'Told you we'd sort this out, Bubby.'

I was a pretty average student and, because my results were so bad in high school, Dad refused to pay for another year of schooling and

... he had these short shorts that would put Britney Spears to shame! Mum even threw them out once and bought him new ones, and good old Dad went to the bin and grabbed the old ones out.

said it was time to get a job. I started working full-time when I was seventeen and have never looked back. He also always encouraged me to study something, anything, even if it wasn't applicable to what I was aiming towards, just to keep growing my knowledge. After years of studying and going back to university part-time as an adult student (while working full-time), I got my diploma. It was the best advice ever.

Later, he gave me the worst advice ever: when we walked into the church the day of my wedding, before he walked me down the aisle, he said,

'Bubby, it's never too late to change your mind.' I can't say I was impressed.

We had some other difficult conversations over the years, but the hardest was when he thought he may have a daughter from a previous relationship. The conversation was probably harder for my dad than me because he had painted this image of himself being good, wholesome and a true family man and he was terrified to tell me and Mum. When Dad met his 'daughter', he knew straight away she was not his and she knew he was not her dad, so it was back to just Dad, Mum and me — us three.

Don't skimp on the classics. There are certain things you shouldn't fudge on no matter how cheaply you dress: the very best boots, a sturdy bag, a glorious jacket or shirt.

Caterine Milinaire and Carol Troy, from *Cheap Chic: Hundreds of Money-Saving Hints to Create Your Own Great Look*, originally published in 1975

Awkward Conversations

Have you ever noticed how parents can go from the most wonderful people in the world to totally embarrassing in three seconds?

Rick Riordan, from *The Red Pyramid*

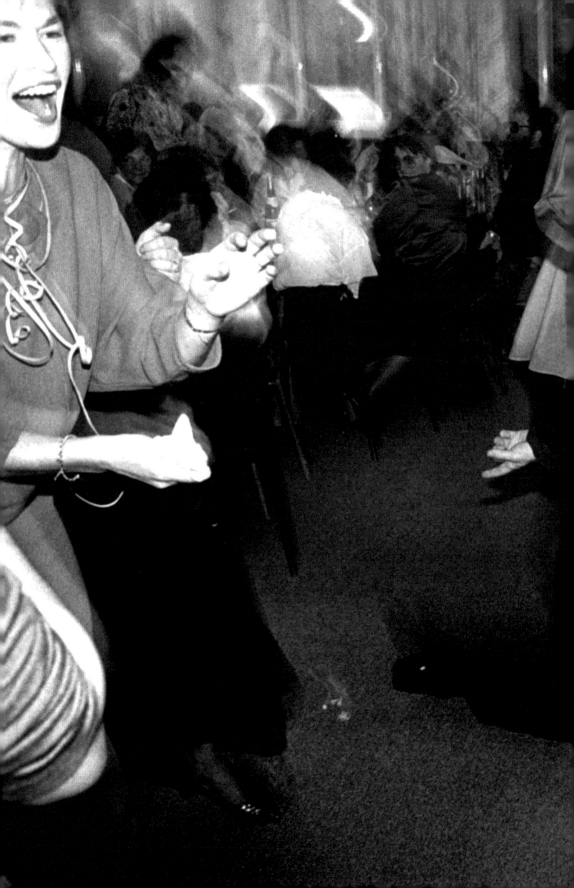

'I'm going to milk the groove and make some tasty shakes!' boomed Dad the MC, rocking the mic. Nat died a little bit inside.

Nigel Smith, from *Nathalia Buttface and the Most Embarrassing Dad in the World*

Where do babies come from? Don't bother asking adults. They lie like pigs. However, diligent independent research and hours of playground consultation have yielded fruitful, if tentative, results. There are several theories. Near as we can figure out, it has something to do with acting ridiculous in the dark. We believe it is similar to dogs when they act peculiar and ride each other. This is called 'making love'. Careful study of popular song lyrics, advertising catchlines, TV sitcoms, movies, and T-Shirt inscriptions offers us significant clues as to its nature. Apparently it makes grown-ups insipid and insane. Some graffiti was once observed that said 'sex is good'.
All available evidence, however, points to the contrary.

Matt Groening

I was eighteen and about to go off to college, and so one day he summoned me into his bathroom. 'Close the door,' he said. 'I have to ask you something.'

'What, Dad?'

'Do you . . . clean your navel?'

'Uh, no.'

'Well, you should. You're a man now, and you sweat, and sweat can collect in your navel and produce an odour that is very . . . offensive.' Then: 'This is witch hazel. It eliminates odours. This is a Q-Tip. To clean your navel, just dip the Q-Tip into the witch hazel and then swab the Q-Tip around your navel. For about thirty seconds. You don't have to do it every day; just once a week or so.' He demonstrated the technique on himself, then handed me my own Q-Tip.

'But, Dad, who is going to smell my navel?'

'You're going off to college, son. You're going to meet women. You never want to risk turning them off with an offensive odour.'

Tom Junod, from 'My Father's Fashion Tips'

I wanted to ask my father about his regrets. I wanted to ask him what was the worst thing he'd ever done. His greatest sin. I wanted to ask him if there was any reason why the Catholic Church would consider him for sainthood. I wanted to open up his dictionary and find the definitions for faith, hope, goodness, sadness, tomato, son, mother, husband, virginity, Jesus, wood, sacrifice, pain, foot, wife, thumb, hand, bread and sex.

'Do you believe in God?' I asked my father.

'God has lots of potential,' he said.

'When you pray,' I asked him. 'What do you pray about?'

'That's none of your business,' he said.

We laughed.

Sherman Alexie, from 'One Good Man'

Daughter: Dad, where do babies come from?

Me: They are dropped off by storks flying through the sky. You were dropped off by one named Marvin.

Brian A. Klems, from

Oh Boy, You're Having a Girl

It was pretty crappy,
I came home from a
birthday party and
he had moved out.
It was pretty abrupt.

Jennifer Aniston

'Dad' Texts

You left your phone at home

There is lightly fried fish fillets for dinner

Dad it's 1 15 am wtf

Do you want the lightly fried fish fillets or not?

Well I mean yea

Mhm thought so come downstairs they're still hot

Wait why did you just make them?

Yes I wasn't tired so I decided to make some lightly fried fish fillets

Say lightly fried fillets one more time dad

Hey sweetie

Hey dad, wanna play the truth game

Sure

I'm pregnant

Your brother crashed your car :)

In a meeting

In a meeting

In a meeting

In a meeting

In a meeting

In a meeting

In a meeting

Are you in a meeting?

No, why?

I had to actually come out to
my dad three times before he
acknowledged it. I'm not sure if
maybe he was hoping he heard it
wrong, like I said, 'Dad, I'm grey.'

Mitchell Pritchett, in *Modern Family*

I think the best thing to try to do is allow your daughter or your son to know that they can come to you for anything. If you can break down that wall so they don't feel embarrassed by telling you things, that's half the battle.

Variously attributed to both Jamie Foxx and Channing Tatum

In high school, when a boy would call and my dad happened to answer, he'd yell upstairs, without even covering the receiver, 'Sarah! There's some mouth breather on the phone for you!' When my first boyfriend drove me to our first formal dance, and all the parents were taking pictures beforehand, my dad pulled my boyfriend aside, put his hand on his shoulder, and said, 'Andy, keep your eyes on the road and your hands on the wheel.' And it worked. The kid was too scared to slow dance.

Sarah Brown

Kirsten Fleming

37, journalist, New York City, USA

I grew up in Jackson, New Jersey, and I live in Manhattan but my dad, Andrew Joseph Fleming, was from the Bronx. He was a complicated man who grew up with an alcoholic father, and he did everything in his power to provide the childhood he never had. He died eight years ago, at fifty-nine.

He was tough but attentive. He loved sports and made sure we did too. But he was a stubborn bastard. Once a pizzeria sent him the wrong order and, when they didn't offer to fix it, he slapped 'The Ban' on that pizzeria. As a family we could never go there again. We called him Dandy Andy because he was the opposite of light and dandy. He could be cranky as all hell.

I was a teenage athlete and played basketball and soccer during my high-school years. My friends told me to try out for cheerleading because I could jump. When I told him I was going to be a cheerleader, he told me that I 'had rocks in my head' and should go out for cross-country instead. I went out for cross-country and became an obsessive long-distance runner. When I was really little, he would jog a few miles to keep in shape and I would try to keep up with him. So, when he forced me to run

cross-country, I had no idea I would become a runner. When I crossed the finish line of my first marathon in 2002, he was there beaming and taking photos. He grinned like a clown. He was so proud. And he knew he was the reason I became a runner in the first place. He let me lean on him as we walked around the field together afterwards, keeping me loose as I cooled down. There was no one else I wanted to share that moment with.

He gave bad advice too. When I quit my job in Boston and my best friend and I went to Costa Rica for a month, he didn't talk to me for weeks; he thought it was terrible that I travelled without a job. But I learned so much about myself and figured out that I wanted to write for a living.

When my father was diagnosed with terminal cancer, he didn't want to talk at all. But he started his chemotherapy in December, and at Christmas he and I stayed up late at night watching a John Wayne marathon including *The Shootist*, which is about a terminally ill man going out on his terms. He told me how chemo wasn't that bad and he felt like he was going to live for a while. I know he hadn't really opened up to anyone so, as much as it was painful to talk about, I was happy he did.

We called him Dandy Andy because he was the opposite of light and dandy. He could be cranky as all hell.

Late Notes

Utah-based dad Seth King regularly writes imaginatively awkward notes to his children's school teachers and posts them on Instagram

Please excuse Isabella for her tardiness. We, as a family, had a difficult time this morning casting roles for our a.m. production of "The Sound of Music". She wanted the role of Captain Von Trap and clearly she would be a better Brigita.
Thanks. ♥ Seth King

Please excuse Sophia for being late We were up late last night making our halloween (All Hallows Eve™) costumes and preparing our musical numbers/dramatic scenes to go with them. We are going to all be Cats from CATS: The Musical™ and in lieu of saying 'trick-or-treat' we shall grace each house with a snippet of that one-of-a-kind, long-running Broadway musical. Our neighbors are in for a treat, errrr... a musical treat!
Tender Hugs, Seth King
#IWANTTOBEMAGICALMRMESTOPHOLES
#SOPHIAPRETENDSTOHATEHERPARENTS
#WEARESUPERHIP

Please excuse Isabella for being late. We were up late celebrating Columbus Day. In honor of the day we (as a family) went across our street to the neighbors house, occupied it, and claimed it as our own. We had a blast; although our neighbors weren't exactly "thrilled", LOL. When we let them back upstairs after having locked them in their basement we had a little explaining to do.
Hugs, Seth King
#reallifehistorylessons #worldsworstholiday
#buyingagiftbasketfortheneighbors

Please excuse Carson for being late this morning. He was busy writing a song about rainbows for his grandmother, then he braided his sisters hair and baked us all cinnamon rolls. He's an angel.
#teenageboys Hugs, Seth King

Please excuse Isabella for being late. But maybe she wasn't late... maybe YOU were early. Maybe the concept of time only exists in our minds so we as humans believe something drives us forward outside ourselves... Hmmmmmm.

Seth King

Please excuse Nolan for being late. He was rummaging through his Dad's music collection and decided that N.W.A.'s "Straight Outta Compton" was a good choice for music to start his day. We had to have a very frank discussion on 'school appropriate' and 'school inappropriate' words.

Hugs,
Seth King

#straightouttaHerrimancrazyfirstgradernamedNolan
#hesotinkingsmartyeahhisbrainsallswollen
#doeshishomework #notaschooljerk
#hisfavoritedancemoveisadeepsquatslowtwerk

Rapped to the cadence/song 'straight outta compton' first stanza.

Please excuse Sophia for being late. She was trying to shove almonds into the paper shredder to make homemade Almond butter... unsuccessfully. She refuses to eat anything processed after watching the documentary "FED UP™" due to the "hidden amounts of sugar in everything"... Alas, we appreciate her health-minded intensity.

Hugs,
Seth King

#SOPIAISSUGARFREE
#Sethnotsomuchbuttrying

Please excuse Carson for being absent. He was with his wildly popular boyband "Essence of Pubescence™" in the studio putting the finishing touches on their Irish-themed, St. Patty's day-centric album. Some of the featured songs:

• "You Lepre-conned My Heart"
• "Pot O' Cold" (AKA Post Break-up)
• "You're Me Lucky Charm"
• "Let's Darby O' Chill"
• "Finnegan's Wake... Board"
• "Choco Milk in the Jar" (to the tune of "Whiskey in the Jar")
• "Top of the Mornin' to you"
• "Just Pinch Me" (AKA Not Wearing Green on Purpose)

They are hoping to get the album released before the Irish Holiday so it was a necessary recording session. Hugs, Seth

#blueeyesthatharmonize #Irishrootsarestrongwiththisone #O'BoyleRULES

Teuila Blakely

41, actor & writer, Auckland, New Zealand

Dad was born in 1938, in Kokonga, a tiny town in Central Otago. His parents came from big Otago farming families; staunch Catholics. His name is Francis Avery Blakely, but people call him Frank.

He left school at fourteen to help his father full-time on the farm. Then he came up to Tokoroa to work in forestry. In Tokoroa, he met a Samoan man at work, who set him up with his niece, my mum, Martha, in 1963. She was a nursing student living in Auckland. Dad says he took one look at her and it was love at first sight. They were married in December 1965 in St Joseph's church in Grey Lynn. Mum, being German-Samoan and Mormon, didn't go down too well with his family at first.

They were both quite entrepreneurial, so they sold their home in Auckland,

moved to Tauranga and bought a takeaway bar. Later, they bought a second shop. We lived out in Welcome Bay, but I grew up in those takeaway shops.

I am the fourth of five kids born to my parents (my parents later went on to adopt another child twenty years younger than me). Although some of my happiest memories were when we would go and visit my grandparents at their farm, they were very set in their belief that interracial marriages didn't work. I used to think that they seemed racist, but it really was what they believed, and, considering the backgrounds they came from, I understand it.

We were no strangers to racism growing up in Tauranga in the 1970s. Dad was the one who taught me that just because other people looked down on us because of the colour of our skin, we didn't have to feel ashamed.

My parents didn't have the smoothest of marriages because of their cultural and religious differences. Of course, love is love, but certainly there's a lot more to it. Dad was always the softy, the nurturer. Mum was a ruthless disciplinarian and not particularly maternal. She would work long hours with Dad at the shops. She'd also go away a lot to Samoa to look after her family estate, so Dad, for much of our lives, was our primary parent.

Until I started school, he would take me to the takeaway shop with him every morning. I'd ride my trike in the shop while Dad would set up. I would tag along like a little shadow and we would talk and talk and talk.

Between the ages of twelve and sixteen, my mum was away in Samoa quite a lot. It's vital for a young girl to have a mother in those years, and I was going through things I couldn't share with Dad — puberty, boys, et cetera. I ended up pregnant at sixteen, partly because I didn't have anyone guiding me.

When I finally told my parents, I was four months' pregnant. I had one more year of high school left to complete and was doing well, with a plan to study law. But with the disappointment that I brought to the family, thanks to our culture and religion, Mum disowned me, and I had to move out right there, on the spot.

That was heartbreaking. It was so difficult. One of the hardest parts was seeing how hurt my dad was. I knew how much he loved me, and how much potential he knew I had. It was my dad who talked my mum and the rest of the family, who were all staunch Mormons,

into allowing me back home. When my son, Jared, was three months old, Mum went back to Samoa and would only see him twice in the next ten years.

With my son's own father not in the picture at all, Dad was the only father figure for Jared in his first three years of life. By this time, Dad was working for Suburban Newspapers, delivering newspapers in bulk. Hard work. I was out working long hours to make ends meet, so Dad would put my son in the car seat and take him around with him while delivering newspapers, and when they got home he'd look after Jared while he tended his garden.

Jared was Dad's only grandchild for ten years, so their bond is very special and unbreakable. They're so close and I'm such a daddy's girl that, when I was finally in a position for us to move out on our own, we moved to the house next door.

Dad's an incredibly patient man and I've never heard him say a bad word about anyone — in fact, he's the only person I ever remember saying anything kind to me as a child. He's completely influenced how I am as a person. He truly does not judge anyone and it's always been second nature to me to not judge as well. He has always been so incredibly proud of me. It's unconditional; it wouldn't make a difference what I did for a living.

Now, I see Mum and Dad once or twice a week or whenever I can. I am very conscious that he's nearing the end of his life. He's always laboured hard, so his body's frail, but otherwise he's good. On his birthday or Father's Day, I'll take him shopping, because he doesn't spend a lot on himself, and he loves it. We still like to talk and talk and talk.

I wondered what my father had
looked like that day, how he had felt,
marrying the lively and beautiful
girl who was my mother. I wondered
what his life was like now. Did he
ever think of us? I wanted to hate
him, but I couldn't; I didn't know
him well enough. Instead, I wondered
about him occasionally, with a
confused kind of longing. There was
a place inside me carved out for him;
I didn't want it to be there, but it was.
Once, at the hardware store, Brooks
had shown me how to use a drill.
I'd made a tiny hole that went deep.
The place for my father was like that.

Elizabeth Berg, from *We Are All Welcome Here*

First Lesson

The first thing to remember about fathers is, they're men.
A girl has to keep it in mind.
They are dragon-seekers, bent on impossible rescues.
Scratch any father, you find
Someone chock-full of qualms and romantic terrors,
Believing change is a threat –
Like your first shoes with heels on, like your first bicycle
It took such months to get.

Walk in strange woods, they warn you about the snakes there.
Climb and they fear you'll fall.
Books, angular boys, or swimming in deep water –
Fathers mistrust them all.
Men are the worriers. It is difficult for them
To learn what they must learn:
How you have a journey to take and very likely,
For a while, will not return.

Phyllis McGinley

Alma Vaitkunskaite

38, stay-at-home mother, Dubai, United Arab Emirates

My father, Vincas Vaitkunskas, was born in a small village with sixty houses and not more than 200 people, called Juncionys. It was just after World War II, when Lithuania belonged to the Soviet Union. I was born in Alytus, Lithuania, forty kilometres from his birthplace and where he now lives. He's seventy. He's a husband and a father of two daughters, me and my sister, Egle.

He worked a lot, repairing the bodywork on cars, when we were children, but our weekends were very active. We lived in an apartment, so we would go camping and fishing in the summer and in the fall we took long walks down the river. In the winter, we'd go skiing.

He was and is a perfectionist. He taught me to always keep trying, not to leave unfinished work. He doesn't have a high education or a degree, but the standards of his work were always very high. As children, living and being with him, it was very hard to make a mistake. He was very harsh on himself and he always required the same from others. We had to do things perfectly from the beginning. He would help us, but we were not allowed to make mistakes. He's very kind inside, but even playtime or drawing had to be perfect and arranged properly. Timing was very strict. I remember feeling very tight in my own skin because of this.

I trained to be a doctor of radiology. Then I met my husband online. The relationship started as friends, but after two years the relationship was very deep and we moved forward and got engaged. The hardest conversation I ever had with my dad was when I had to inform him that I was getting married to a Muslim. He grew up in a time when religion was forbidden in the Soviet Union, so it wasn't important in my family, but he was fearful of the stories he saw on the news. He cried.

He is a caring, loving, strict grandfather to my children now, who are nine and six. Every summer, when the kids finish school in June, straight away we go to Lithuania until September. We go to the same lakes I went to as a child. We go fishing. We help him in his garage.

After marrying someone from a different nationality and coming to Dubai — we came for my husband's job eight years ago — I had to become more flexible. Now, no one is required to be perfect anymore. I'm softer on my kids. I don't like unfinished things or people being late, but I don't judge them like I used to.

My father has never been to Dubai and he doesn't want to. My mum came a few times, but my father's not a city type. He likes the forest and nature, and says he can see Dubai on the TV. If he came, he would come for me, but he wouldn't have fun here.

The hardest conversation I ever had with my dad was when I had to inform him that I was getting married to a Muslim.

I'm the cool dad, . . . that's my thang. I'm hip, I surf the web, I text: LOL – laugh out loud; OMG – oh, my god; WTF – why the face. Um, you know, I know all the dances to *High School Musical* . . .

Phil Dunphy, in *Modern Family*

The Measure of a Man

Not – How did he die?
But – How did he live?
Not – What did he gain?
But – What did he give?
These are the things that measure the worth
Of a man as a man, regardless of birth.

Not – What was his station?
But – Had he a heart?
And – How did he play his God-given part?
Was he ever ready with a word of good cheer?
To bring back a smile, to banish a tear?

Not – What was his church?
Not – What was his creed?
But – Had he befriended those really in need?

Not – What did the sketch in the newspaper say?
But – How many were sorry when he passed away?
These are the things that measure the worth
Of a man as a man, regardless of birth.

Anonymous

I can't really watch my dad dance. It's just very uncomfortable for me. I'm just not really feeling it. So I was more into his ballads, because watching my dad dance, I just got so embarrassed.

Nicole Richie on her father, Lionel Richie

Stuart Isett

49, photographer, Seattle, Washington, USA

My father was Robert Lee Isett Jr,
an army brat born in 1935 in Lebanon,
Pennsylvania, but he spent time all
over the USA and in Germany. His dad —
my grandfather — was a US Army colonel
and tank commander who fought in both
World War II and the Korean War.

My dad grew up to be a US Army
Ranger out of college, but he quit
the army in 1963 and took a job in
finance in Zurich, Switzerland, where
I was born. He then moved to London,
where he started his own business,
which was a pretty risky thing to do
in those days. I've always respected
him for that. He sent me and my two
older brothers to British, all-boys
schools, but never tried to keep us
in a bubble.

After almost two decades, our
family returned to the USA. He was
very successful for a while but, by
the time he retired, he lived a very
modest and simple life in Miami,
Florida. He died in October 2014 from
cancer, aged seventy-nine.

My dad was a man of the 1950s: he
missed the entire social revolution
of the sixties and seventies, so he
didn't have much of a modern world
view. He did teach us how to travel
and get around the world, which has
helped in my work as a globetrotting
photographer, but he was distant and
not very close with us. I often wish
he had helped me more to become an
adult. He didn't really engage with
us, which I guess gave us independence
and forced us to learn about the world
by ourselves, but it's something I
won't repeat with my kids.

One of my fondest memories of him
is the time he let me climb up on him

while he was sitting in his leather
chair. I was probably eight years old
and it was one of the last times he
was ever physical with me in that way.
My brother owns that chair now and I
have a hard time looking at it because
my father was an alcoholic and, in my
teen years, very verbally combative
and argumentative. There were too many
arguments and difficult conversations.
I believe he was much more sensitive
and emotional than a man of his
generation was allowed to be and that
it was this dichotomy and conflict
that caused him a lot of problems.

In his later years he was a cultural
recluse. He enjoyed his food and
travel, but didn't really engage with
the world. It reminds me of that old
Bob Dylan line, 'He ain't busy being
born, he's busy dying'. But I think
he found comfort living like that,
because by then the world was a bit
too much for him.

I got along fine with him later
in life because he stopped drinking.
But only from a distance — being one
on one with him for any extended
period of time was still tough.

He was good grandfather; always
remembered the kids' birthdays, sent
them little gifts for Easter and
Halloween every year. He made up,
in a way, for not being such a good
father by being a good grandfather.
And, in his last few months, he made
up for the many years of problems we
had had. His wife had died and he had
Alzheimer's, but he did everything
we asked of him without complaint,
including moving across the country
to be near one of my brothers. While
he was confused, he didn't complain

or resist and it made our last months with him pretty easy.

I have two daughters: Zoe, who is ten, and Phoebe, who is five. I'm different from him in some ways — I engage with my kids, am involved in their lives and help to shape their world views but, like my dad, I try to teach them to travel, be adventurous and not afraid to take risks. As a freelance photographer, I get to spend a lot of time with my kids — way more than my father ever did. I'm working at home most days, so I take the kids to school and pick them up, take them to doctor and dentist appointments, play dates, et cetera. My wife doesn't get to do all this stuff because she has a regular nine-to-five job, but I think it works for us.

I like to challenge my kids, keep them on their toes. I'm probably too tough on them — patience would be a virtue, if I had more — but their mother's kindness is a good balance and I want my kids to question everything around them. Here in Seattle, there's a lot of political and cultural conformity, so I want my kids to always be wary of what their elders say. I try to teach them to defend their ideas by challenging them, and I want them to be competitive. I don't want my girls to be soft or weak.

My kids humour me, especially the younger one. My dad's sayings were numerous and really defined him. He'd say things like, 'Bullshit baffles brains.' I use his quips all the time now, and my kids roll their eyes.

. . . he was distant and not very close with us. I often wish he had helped me more to become an adult.

On the self-abuse front – and this is important – I don't think it's advisable to do it in the shower. It wastes water and electricity and because we all expect you to be doing it there in any case. And, not on . . . under the linen . . . Well . . . Anyway, if you're worried about anything at all, just feel free to ask and we'll look it up.

Ben Hood, in *The Ice Storm*

Alas, raising
a young lady
is a mystery
even beyond an
enchanter's skill.

Lloyd Alexander, from *The Castle of Llyr*

Mpho A. Tutu van Furth

53, episcopal priest, Cape Town, South Africa

I was born in England. We returned to South Africa when I was about three years old. South Africa was so different.

A few years ago, I was with my father in the Eastern Cape. As we went past this park in East London, my dad said, 'You wanted to go and play in there and I had to tell you no. And you said "Why?" I had to tell you that it wasn't for children like you.' He had the challenge of having to explain apartheid to a three-year-old. I think that it was confusing to me. I couldn't see the difference between those children and me. They were just children playing in the park. They were children like the friends I had had in England. I couldn't figure out what it was about them that was so different . . . As I think about it, and as I think about the people who I have come to call friends over the course of my life, I would have to say that, whatever it was that he said or however it was that he explained it to me, I didn't walk away having written off a race of people for the stupidity of some.

I am an episcopal priest. I studied and was ordained in the United States. When I got to seminary, I found out that my father was ubiquitous: he'd written the foreword for this text, the afterword for that text, and he was quoted in another text, and his speech is excerpted in yet another text.

I'm not sure whether it was a pain or an inspiration. It was a curiosity. I think I had taken him much more lightly than was warranted. I think that as I engaged in my own theological studies, and found him quoted and excerpted all over the place, I recognised him as much more of a heavyweight than I had given him credit for.

He wears his accomplishments very lightly. He's not the person who is constantly hammering you over the head with his achievements and what he's managed to do against the odds. He doesn't assault you with what it is that you have to live up to; that is not at all who he is. He was incredibly respectful of my process. He let me find my way, the way I needed to. When I told my mother that I wanted to go to seminary and I wanted to become a priest, my mum was a mum: she was thrilled and enthusiastic and excited. My dad prayed with me.

The day that I graduated from seminary at the Episcopal Divinity School in Cambridge, Massachusetts, my father was the commencement speaker at Virginia Theological Seminary in Alexandria, Virginia. He had agreed to the engagement before he knew my graduation date. I was really disappointed that he wasn't going to be with me, but I had made peace with it. My mum was going to be there and that was wonderful. He called me the morning of my graduation to apologise again and I was trying to be really fine, although I wasn't really, really fine. I didn't want to make him feel bad, because he was doing what he had to do. At the beginning of the ceremony, all the graduates marched in and then we were all seated. Suddenly I heard a small rush of

sound like waves on pebbles. I turned around and my dad was getting into the seat next to my mother. She was as surprised as I was. He had made his speech and jumped off the podium, run to a waiting car, got a flight to Boston, got a police escort from the airport to the chapel to come and be at my graduation.

He's not just a father: he is a daddy. He says so.

When my older sister celebrated her fiftieth birthday my father and I celebrated the Eucharist. We had shared the liturgy before, but on those times one of us was preaching and the other presiding. This time we presided together and for me it was lovely — more than lovely. It was amazing and sacred and wonderful and all of those things. But afterwards I had an additional piece of context. I had a conversation afterwards with Brigalia Bam. She had argued for the ordination of women at the provincial synod that finally decided to ordain women to the priesthood in South Africa. She spoke about how important that was. She and others talked about how hard my father had worked for women's ordination and how he had prayed for it. She said, 'He never knew when he was struggling for the right of women to become priests that one of the outcomes would be that he would one day be able to stand at the altar with his own daughter and concelebrate the Eucharist.' That, in retrospect, made the moment even more momentous.

He had the challenge of having to explain apartheid to a three-year-old.

I never saw my dad cry. My son saw me cry.
My dad never told me he loved me, and
consequently I told Scott I loved him every
other minute. The point is, I'll make less
mistakes than my dad, my sons hopefully will
make less mistakes than me, and their sons
will make less mistakes than their dads.

James Caan

Dad was sitting with feet up on the settee watching a late film. 'You shouldn't be watching this,' I told him. 'It's rude.'

'I close my eyes when the naughty bits come on.'

Berlie Doherty, from *Dear Nobody*

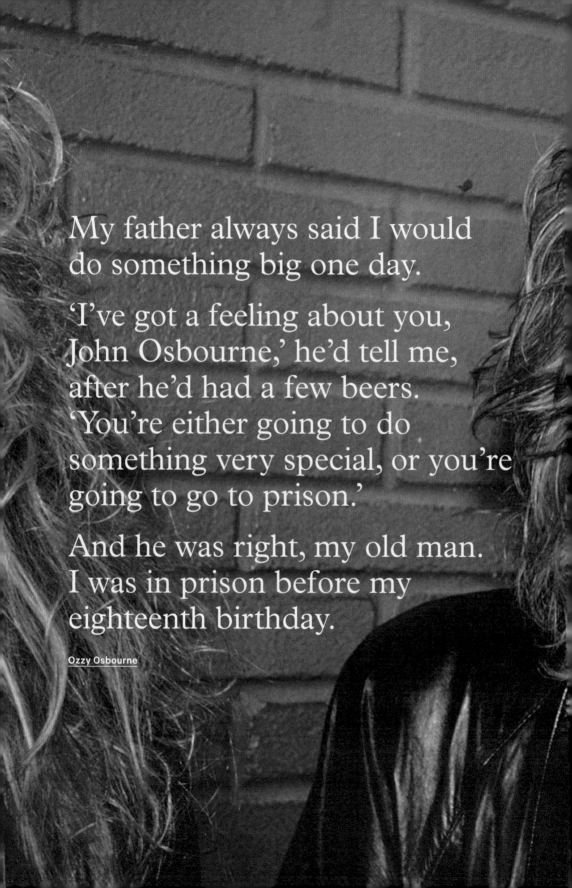

My father always said I would do something big one day.

'I've got a feeling about you, John Osbourne,' he'd tell me, after he'd had a few beers. 'You're either going to do something very special, or you're going to go to prison.'

And he was right, my old man. I was in prison before my eighteenth birthday.

Ozzy Osbourne

I could have asked my father lots of questions. I could have. But there was something in his face and eyes and in his crooked smile that prevented me from asking. I guess I didn't believe he wanted me to know who he was. So I just collected clues . . . Some day all the clues would come together. And I would solve the mystery of my father.

Benjamin Alire Sáenz, from *Aristotle and Dante Discover the Secrets of the Universe*

We were in Montgomery and I couldn't
read the sign saying 'White Only' and
'Coloured Only' . . . I ran up and went to a
water fountain. Well, as I came back from
the fountain there four guys came and
were harassing my dad and I kept thinking
to myself, 'These guys better calm down
because my dad is going to kick their
ass. Because I know Dad. He's
a military guy and he takes no mess.'

And Dad didn't say a word, and it
bothered me from nine years old until
I was twenty-two. Then I remember saying
to my dad one day, 'Why didn't you kick
their ass? You turned and cowardly
walked away.'

And he had the greatest line ever. He
said to me, 'I had a choice that day of
either being a man or your father. I knew
if I fought them they would kill me, and
I chose to be your dad.'

Lionel Richie

Sam Mannering

29, restaurateur, food writer & actor, Auckland, New Zealand

My father, Roger Mannering, is a dairy farmer. He grew up in the Waikato. His father was a military man, through and through. Precise, old school and proper as you like. Incredibly dapper and well spoken and well read. A perfect gentleman. Dad's not really like that at all. You see elements of it — the way he holds a knife and fork — but he's very much a man's man, a rugby player, very blokey.

Dad was twenty-six when I was born. He and my mother married at twenty-five, and it was a bit of a cliché — he was the best man at a wedding; she was back from Scotland for six weeks and at the wedding. She had been living in Scotland for a couple of years, but she never returned after that.

I was born in the Waikato and lived there on a farm till I was about eight or nine. Then we moved to Canterbury. I'm the oldest and we're a bit like the Von Trapps — we're all three years apart. There are four of us — three boys and my sister, who's the youngest. Dad has never called any of us by our names. He'll call me Fred or Horace. He'll call Mum George. My sister goes by Myrtle, Tinkerbell, Fluffy or Flossy. He's always been Podge — or Podgey.

We grew up roaming, really: fishing, getting into trouble, hanging out with the calves, building huts in the hay sheds. There Dad was, getting the tractor in, creating these amazing hay-bale forts we'd spend weeks in. If he was near, you knew nothing would go wrong. He's six foot four and got these huge farmer's hands and he envelops you in a hug. But you also would never mess with him.

He's always been a shrewd businessman. When we moved to Canterbury, we were surrounded by crop farmers and scrubby little farms. He saw the opportunity in dairy farming and he jumped on this new world of opportunity when no one was doing it. You give him a project, and he's on it.

When I did my first cookbook, he had reservations. It was hard for him to understand, as it's not a conventional career. But he had my best interests at heart. He's never worked in hospitality and it's not the way his mind works, but the amount of support and advice he's given me when starting my own café — man. He's very practical and considered and will take things one step at a time. Things have to be thought about, and there has to be a process.

He's certainly a person of his generation. When he gets talking about music, it's all about the eighties — people like Talking Heads, the Finns, Van Morrison. He's also had a moustache for as long as Mum's known him, since '79 or '80, and still now at the age of fifty-six. We've always given him stick about it, but it's really grown on me. As a teenager, I'd think, 'Why can't you shave it off?' but now it's just a part of him.

The hardest conversation we ever had? Definitely about me being gay. I was twelve or thirteen when I knew, so I'd known for ten years before I told him. Going to a boarding school, where everything's quite traditional, there was no need or want to confront that particular aspect of my life. So, I went through my teens shelving it, thinking, 'What is my rugby-playing, dairy-farming father going to say about this?' Then it became very apparent, so I went to stay at the farm and spoke to Mum about it. We had a bit of an argument about who I was seeing and there was tension in the air.

The next day, he approached me in the kitchen. 'Right,' he said. 'Your mother's a bit concerned you're feeling beside yourself about the fact you'd rather chase boys than girls. That's ridiculous. We love you regardless.'

Then he hugged me and walked off. It was one of the most gratifying conversations of my life. For him to be so nonchalant about it was unbelievably cathartic. The way he talked about it made me feel OK about it. It wasn't a big deal and he didn't make it a big deal. Nothing more needed to be said.

Ever since, there's nothing I'm not able to tell him. That was the one secret I'd kept from him, and after that, there was nothing between us.

We grew up roaming, really: fishing, getting into trouble, hanging out with the calves, building huts in the hay sheds. There Dad was, getting the tractor in, creating these amazing hay-bale forts we'd spend weeks in.

My darlings . . .

The dream of every family is to live happily together in a quiet and peaceful home where parents will have the opportunity of bringing up the children in the best possible way, or guiding and helping them in choosing careers and of giving them the love and care which will develop in them a feeling of security and self-confidence.

Nelson Mandela in a letter to his daughters, Zindzi and Zenani Mandela,

written on Robben Island, 1 June 1970

Parental Guidance Recommended

If in doubt, go without. Which applies to clothes, one-night stands, tequila shots and takeaway food.

Sam de Brito

I have found the best way to give advice to your children is
to find out what they want and then advise them to do it.

Harry S. Truman

The BUCK STOPS here!

Gareth James

41, museum manager, Glasgow, Scotland

Frederick Blair James is my father. He's known as Blair and is seventy-two. He's lived his whole life in Glasgow, where he was a civil servant for the Department of Social Security for the forty-one years of his working life. Post-retirement, he works as a part-time tour guide at the Scottish Football Museum.

He met my mother in Portballintrae, in Northern Ireland, when they were teenagers, and they have now been married for over fifty years.

My father has never been a sage. He's almost too reticent to offer a definitive opinion on anything. But he is fond of reminding me, whenever I've been moaning about having a shite day at work, that 'work is a four-letter word'. And he has influenced my personality, which has informed the way I am as a parent now.

He's a pretty regular kind of guy with really eclectic taste in music. He'd listen to anything me and my brothers were playing at home and we'd go to gigs at the Barrowland Ballroom in Glasgow to hear live music. My favourite gig was when we went to see David Byrne in 1989. My dad had been blown away by David Byrne and Talking Heads when we went to a screening of *Stop Making Sense* at the Glasgow Film Theatre, so he leapt at the chance of seeing Byrne and his band live. In between songs, my dad asked me, 'What's that curry smell?' I knew it was someone smoking a joint (you could still smoke in venues back then), but as a fifteen-year-old I couldn't admit to my dad that I knew what the illegal aroma was!

Dad bought me a drum kit when I was twelve, and he and my mum (and our neighbours) suffered years of my bad drumming in the attic, as then I moved on to congas, bongos, timbales and lots of other hand percussion. Eventually, he got to see me play gigs in some pretty big venues in Glasgow, like The Old Fruitmarket. I was in bands called Fly, Wisermiserdemelza, Co-Intel-Pro and Imperfect Product, and we played mainly instrumental jazz funk. Although he was bemused at the strange pubs and clubs we played in, I think he was proud. I have a mental picture of him sipping an Irn-Bru through a neon-pink straw from a neon-green plastic highball glass at some dodgy club we played a battle of the bands at.

In our family, and in particular with my dad, we don't talk about our emotions or how we feel. I have only ever seen my dad cry once — when his father died. I'd never seen him so bereft. I had no way of helping him or really understanding what he was going through. I wish that I had had more emotional intelligence back then to help him with his grief and loss.

I have two girls — Lena, who is four, and Tove, who is two. The most surprising thing to me when I became a parent was the realisation of all the small, unending sacrifices that my parents made for me. As I started to make the same sort of sacrifices — emotional, financial, chrono-logical — that my parents did, I marvelled at the true, huge extent of it. You really do give everything for your kids. And you get it back in

... he is fond of reminding me, whenever I've been moaning about having a shite day at work, that 'work is a four-letter word'.

spades as you see these wee creatures grow and blossom. I want to help nurture them into fantastic, strong women who can do anything they want to and be whoever they want to be.

I cry a lot more easily now I'm a dad. I even cry at some of the kids' programmes that the girls watch. The lack of sleep is the most difficult thing — it seems obvious, but the constant nature of it is physically and emotionally exhausting. We've got two amazing livewires and, as a pal warned me when we had two children relatively close together,

it can feel like you're wrestling two drunk clowns for a large percentage of the time.

What kind of grandparent is my dad? He's sort of hands-on and really dedicated, and spends lots of time picking our two wee girls up from nursery and school, taking them on trips. To help our youngest get to sleep at night when she was smaller, he would lie on the floor of her bedroom, holding her hand through the bars of her cot while she drifted off to sleep. It's one of my favourite memories of him.

Give yourself permission to dream. Fuel your kids' dreams too. Once in a while, that might even mean letting them stay up past their bedtimes.

Randy Pausch

I just owe almost everything to my father and it's passionately interesting for me that the things that I learned in a small town, in a very modest home, are just the things that I believe have won the election.

Margaret Thatcher

Peter FitzSimons
54, broadcaster, Sydney, Australia

My father, Peter McCloy FitzSimons, was the age of many of my friends' grandfathers. He died twenty-odd years ago, but 100 years after he was born, 150 people gathered to honour him.

He trained as an accountant and then, after World War II, he decided to go farming. He farmed right up to the last second of his life, when he died of a massive heart attack suddenly, at seventy-six, while helping a neighbour.

He was a very fine, committed father. He was totally supportive. Every rugby game, he was there. We grew up on an orange farm in Peats Ridge, New South Wales, and he would travel down to Sydney and bring us oranges for half-time.

He wasn't strict, and we basically didn't have many rules; no corporal punishment. There wasn't any playing up by us. You worked on the farm and got on with it, and he led by example. Dad was the king and Mum was the parliament. Mum decided when, where and how it would all happen; she was the guiding force. And he was nominally the head of the household.

When I was playing rugby in France, Mum and Dad went on their first European trip together. We were playing against Toulon. I remember being so exhausted at half-time, thinking I couldn't go on, until I heard my father's voice ring out, 'C'mon, Pete!' I immediately felt stronger.

Dad taught me poetry, good strong family values and community values. Of all the values he gave me, the one I live by the most is to use your time. Time is valuable; I pack a lot into my day and I need to get things done. I don't feel satisfied lying around doing nothing. I learned that from him.

I reckon I'm a pretty good father, but, when I measure the fathering I received to the fathering I give, I fall short. The only thing I outdo him on is demonstrativeness. That's a function of his generation; the graph of his emotions never went up or down. I'm far louder, run cooler and hotter. I'm more authoritarian.

I can often hear my father's voice when I talk to my three kids. He'd always say, 'This is our roof and these are our rules,' and I say that to my kids all the time. We're a different breed, but he was a very good man.

He wasn't strict, and we basically didn't have many rules; no corporal punishment. There wasn't any playing up by us. You worked on the farm and got on with it ...

My Dear Son . . .

If you can't win the scholarship, fight it out
to the end of the examination.

If you can't win your race, at least finish —
somewhere.

If your boat can't win, at least keep
pulling on your oar, even if your eye glazes
and the taste of blood comes into your throat
with every heave.

If you cannot make your five yards in
football, keep bucking the line — never let
up — if you can't see, or hear, keep plugging
ahead! Never quit! If you forget all else I
have said, remember these two words, through
all your life, and come success or failure I
shall proudly think of you as my own dear son.

And so, from the old home-life, farewell,
and Godspeed!

John D. Swain to his son as he began student life

at Yale University, 1908

I'm in politics not in spite
of the fact that I have kids,
but because of the fact that
I have kids, and they keep
me really grounded in, 'Well,
am I doing things that are
meaningful, or am I just sort
of playing the game?'

Justin Trudeau

By the time a man realises that maybe his father was right, he usually has a son who thinks he's wrong.

Charles Wadsworth

Delphine Devictor

31, nutritionist, Marseille, France

My dad, Michel Devictor, is sixty-five years old. He has lived his life in Marseille. He's got two younger brothers and one older sister.

I love my dad's family; it's very tight. You can feel the proper spirit of the family. We don't see each other — the cousins — very often, but the feeling is there. My dad carries on this very strong family thing.

He has always been very proud of his family and the people he loves, and he's not afraid to show it. That's quite rare for a guy of his age. He's the kind of person who makes you feel confident. That's why I'm mostly confident, because of his love for us and his pride. He wouldn't say he loved you — that's hard for French people to say — but he'd show it. You can see and feel that he loves his wife too, just by the way he looks at her. He's a very passionate person. He was the best to grow up with. Because of him, I'm the person I am today.

I've got two older brothers — one half brother and one brother. We grew up in the same house they live in today in Marseille. It's at the bottom of the hills and I'm there all the time. My older brother is my half brother and is on my mum's side, but he always felt the same as my other brother. He's autistic and he was in an institution when I was growing up, so he wasn't here all the time. My dad met my mother and just decided he was going to love the guy and that he was his son. I was never ashamed of my brother growing up, like other kids would be. I never suffered from that because my parents didn't see it as a problem.

I remember Dad shouting at me only twice in my life, when I was a teenager and not very nice. It was very clear where the boundaries were in our house. And I'm the only girl, so he's a softie with me.

What was his best advice? To never keep something in that is bothering you. When I was upset and not talking as a teenager, he would come to me and explain that I could tell him anything. He'd say, 'Just get it out.' Now that I'm thirty-one, I can see it's great advice. If something's bothering you, you need to get it out. I think it comes back to the family thing. We're not the perfect family, but we can always talk to each other.

He's been a genealogist for the past forty years. He discovered this job randomly; I think somebody told him about a guy who looked for heirs. He gave it a shot and he loved the job. He's travelled to many countries to look for heirs to resolve estates. He has this thing about family, so I think that's why he's so good at it. Some of the stories are not fun — kids that have been abandoned by the mum, adopted out — but some stories are quite nice. And it's a very interesting job.

My dad offered me a job a few years ago. It was easy and hard to work together. It's a very family company, so I knew everybody there — that was easy. But it's complicated to work with family. And I realised quite quickly it wasn't my passion. My dad was really glad I was working with him, so I guess that put a lot of pressure on me. My brother works with him as well, so when we'd have

dinner we'd talk only about work. It wasn't very pleasant. After two years working with him I decided to go back to school and become a nutritionist.

Telling him I didn't want to work with him anymore was the hardest thing I have ever had to do. He didn't understand it at first. He was like, 'C'mon, why do you want to do that? You have security, insurance, good pay.' As a parent, you always want your children to be safe, and I had that with the job, but I didn't want it. After a while, he got it. And the only thing my dad wants for me is to be happy.

I'm very similar to him in the way I think. We're on the same page; my basic character is like my dad's. We both love travelling; talking to people. We're dynamic. I've done the things he always wanted to do,

including living abroad. He took me to the airport when I left to study in Australia at twenty-two. He was sending his daughter away on her own and he was freaking out, really freaking out. But then he came to Australia to visit and I remember him being happy and very proud of me for doing that.

When I see him now, my dad is very much about food and so am I. We have dinner or lunch. Usually we just chat. I like to hike with both Mum and Dad in the Alps. He's officially retired but he still works two or three days a week. For a few months he was a pain in the ass because he was so into his job and his career. But now he's in a rhythm. He likes to be in the garden. He likes to do crosswords and he's very good at them. He's better. He's found his balance.

What was his best advice? To never keep something in that is bothering you ... He'd say, 'Just get it out.'

Now, Jack,

I don't want to give the impression
that I am a nagger, for goodness knows
I think that is the worst thing any
parent can be, and I also feel that you
know if I didn't really feel you had the
goods I would be most charitable in my
attitude towards your failings. After
long experience in sizing up people I
definitely know you have the goods and
you can go a long way . . . It is very
difficult to make up fundamentals that
you have neglected when you were very
young, and that is why I am urging you to
do the best you can. I am not expecting
too much, and I will not be disappointed
if you don't turn out to be a real
genius, but I think you can be a really
worthwhile citizen with good judgement
and understanding.

Joseph P. Kennedy Sr to his son

John at boarding school, 1934

'Your problem, son, is you're a baritone who thinks he's a tenor.'
With this impeccable one-liner my father, Brendan Robert
Hewson, or Bob as he was universally known, nailed me.

Bono

Dear Charles . . .

I have just had a letter from Aunty
Joan asking whether you received a
Christmas present from her. As in other
matters of life, you are childishly
idle about writing letters, thereby
giving the impression that you are both
ill-mannered and ungrateful. If people
bother to give you a present, the least
they can expect is that you rouse
yourself from your customary state of
squalid inertia and write and say thank
you. I am very fond of you but you do
drive me around the bend.

Roger Mortimer to his son
Charles at boarding school, 1969

Wait 'til your father gets home.

Every mother, ever

He was a better person than I am and I am not just saying this to appear modest. My father was one of those people who was born with a great sense of responsibility, far greater and more developed than mine. From the very moment he started going to school, he was a hard worker, very conscientious. I wasn't like that.

Aung San Suu Kyi

Mandy Jacobs

46, ex-banker, Lincoln, England

Boyd Speed McKay is my father. Speed's a family name. His father's mother came from an old fishing family, quite a large, prestigious family in Campbeltown, a very remote fishing town on the west coast of Scotland, and Speed was their surname. He was also a rugby player and quite speedy on the pitch, I believe, but his nickname when he was working was Bones. He's a gentle giant, but if you push him he'll clench his fists and growl. When he'd clench his fists, the bones would crack.

He lived his life in Glasgow, Scotland. He still does. Ours was a very traditional Glasgow family. We were working class; Mum was at home and Dad was always working. He was an electrician, but he's now retired. He worked for the *Daily Record* newspaper and for Goodyear tyre factory. He worked a lot. He was a shift worker, so quite often he wasn't around. He was always helping out friends, neighbours, family around their houses, but at home there were always things — lights, things in the kitchen — that weren't working.

Doing my maths and physics homework with Dad is one of my best memories. He's a very quiet man who doesn't show much emotion, and it was a time we did stuff together. I was relatively clever and he would challenge me when we did my homework. With school, he was always interested in the not-so-good marks, in what had gone wrong. In hindsight, that was because he was aspirational for me and my younger sister.

Every year we'd visit Campbeltown.

Dad's family had a cottage down there that we would spend Easter or summer holidays at. We'd pack up the car and head down. When we arrived, we'd be dying to get out of the car, but Dad always made us drive around the harbour first, where all the fishing boats were, so he could see them. It was a really important thing for him. I can remember endless time on the beach with a gas stove, having cookouts. It was lots and lots of fun.

I had a very difficult relationship with my mother. She was a very angry person when I was younger and a little bit of a tyrant. I was scared of her and I think my dad was too. He too often wanted to keep the peace and didn't intervene as often as he should have. It was a constant cycle of kowtowing to her all the time. When I met my husband, who is such an amazing dad, I saw a relationship that I would have loved to have had with my dad. And, at thirty-nine, I had a falling out with my mum. Dad wanted me to call her because she was making his life miserable, but I had the security to say, 'No, I'm not putting up with this anymore.' Eventually she got in touch and I was able to have the first adult conversation with her in my entire life. We had such a good discussion and we haven't looked back. The dynamic changed and it isn't rocky anymore.

Dad's been seriously ill this year and the dynamic's changed again — it's strengthened my relationship with my mum even more. Now I see them every month. I've been back and forth to Glasgow four times while he's been in hospital.

The best advice he ever gave me is

The best advice he ever gave me is that you can always come home . . . Really, everything changed for me from that point on.

that you can always come home. When I was twenty-three, I was working for an investment firm in Glasgow. I was offered a job with Barings Bank. It meant the opportunity to double my salary instantly, but I had to go to South America for six months. I'd never travelled anywhere on my own before. It was really overwhelming for a working-class girl from Glasgow. Dad told me I could always come home — and that gave me the comfort factor and I went. I camped out in these hotels in South America. It was before mobile phones, so on a Sunday afternoon I'd call

home and let the phone ring two times before hanging up. Mum and Dad would call back with two rings and hang up. Calls were too expensive, so we didn't pick up the phone and talk — it was our way of telling each other we were thinking of each other.

Really, everything changed for me from that point on. My life would have been two-point-four children and a husband in Glasgow. I wouldn't have experienced what I've experienced in life — living in London, meeting my husband. I've seen things that I wouldn't have seen in a million years if I hadn't gone.

In my younger and more vulnerable years my father gave me some advice that I've been turning over in my mind ever since. 'Whenever you feel like criticising anyone,' he told me, 'just remember that all the people in this world haven't had the advantages that you've had.'

F. Scott Fitzgerald, from *The Great Gatsby*

When I was a boy of fourteen, my father was so ignorant I could hardly stand to have the old man around. But when I got to be twenty-one, I was astonished at how much the old man had learned in seven years.

Mark Twain

If

If you can keep your head when all about you
Are losing theirs and blaming it on you,
If you can trust yourself when all men doubt you,
But make allowance for their doubting too;
If you can wait and not be tired by waiting,
Or being lied about, don't deal in lies,
Or being hated, don't give way to hating,
And yet don't look too good, nor talk too wise:

If you can dream – and not make dreams your master;
If you can think – and not make thoughts your aim;
If you can meet with Triumph and Disaster
And treat those two impostors just the same;
If you can bear to hear the truth you've spoken
Twisted by knaves to make a trap for fools,
Or watch the things you gave your life to, broken,
And stoop and build 'em up with worn-out tools:

If you can make one heap of all your winnings
And risk it on one turn of pitch-and-toss,
And lose, and start again at your beginnings
And never breathe a word about your loss;
If you can force your heart and nerve and sinew
To serve your turn long after they are gone,
And so hold on when there is nothing in you
Except the Will which says to them: 'Hold on!'

If you can talk with crowds and keep your virtue,
Or walk with Kings – nor lose the common touch,
If neither foes nor loving friends can hurt you,
If all men count with you, but none too much;
If you can fill the unforgiving minute
With sixty seconds' worth of distance run,
Yours is the Earth and everything that's in it,
And – which is more – you'll be a Man, my son!

Rudyard Kipling

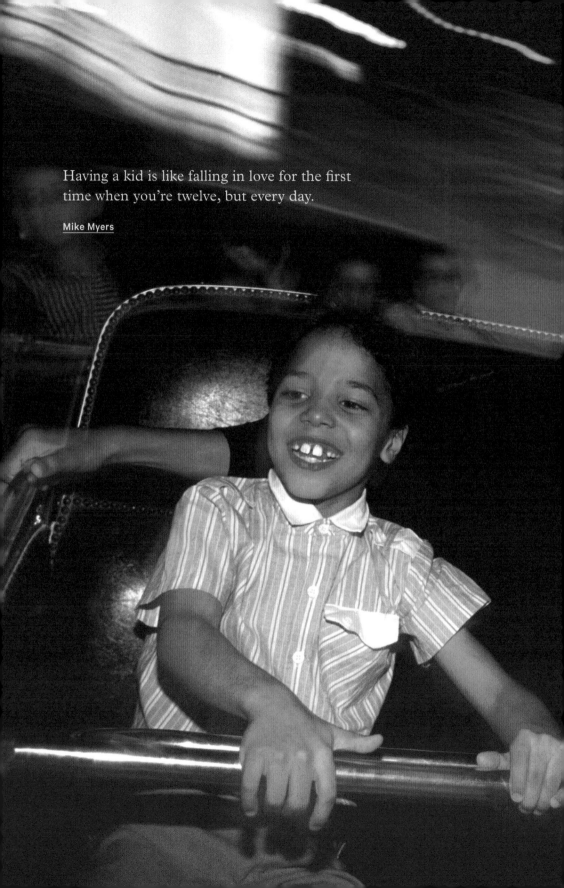

Having a kid is like falling in love for the first time when you're twelve, but every day.

Mike Myers

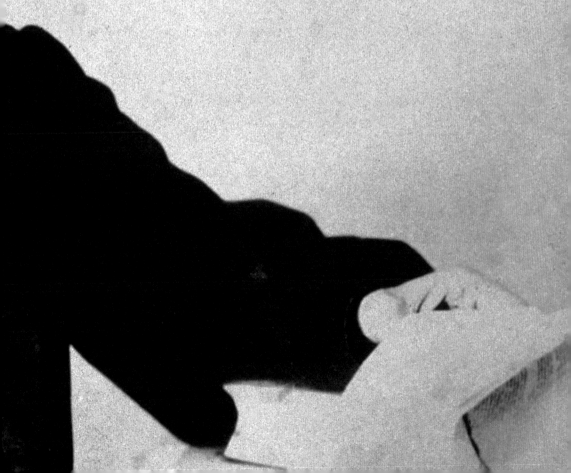

My father taught me to work; he did not teach me to love it.

Abraham Lincoln

My friend was homesick and
got letters from his parents.
His mum's was two pages long.
His dad's just said, 'Be a man.'

Jimmy Fallon

He promised us that everything would be OK. I was a child, but I knew that everything would not be OK. That did not make my father a liar. It made him my father.

Jonathan Safran Foer, from *Extremely Loud and Incredibly Close*

I don't want to exaggerate but, by God, it was a bad wedding. Here I am, at twenty-four, waiting to come down the aisle in my red velvet dress, with ivy in my hair. I look like Lady Bacchus . . . My father is in a suit he shoplifted from Ciro Citterio, and some shoes he shoplifted from Burtons – but he looks calm, wise and not a little emotional about giving away his first child in marriage.

'Oh, my lovely daughter,' he says, smelling a little of whiskey. 'My kitten-cat.' His eyes have the faint shine of tears in them. As the music strikes up in the next room – the slow, village march of The Lilac Time's 'Spin A Cavalu' – he takes my arm, and leans in to whisper something. This is where he tells me something of how he and Mum have stayed together for twenty-four years, and had eight kids, I think to myself. This is going to be one of our great bonding moments. Oh Lord, I hope he doesn't make me cry. I have so much eyeliner on.

'Darling girl,' he says, as the usher opens the door, and I see the whole congregation crane around, to watch my entrance. 'Darling love. Remember you're a Womble.'

Caitlin Moran, from *How to Be a Woman*

**Dear Hildita, Aleidita, Camilo,
Celia and Ernesto,**

If you ever have to read this letter, it
will be because I am no longer with you.
   You practically will not remember me, and
the smaller ones will not remember me at all.
   Your father has been a man who acted on
his beliefs and has certainly been loyal
to his convictions.
   Grow up as good revolutionaries. Study
hard so that you can master technology, which
allows us to master nature. Remember that
the revolution is what is important, and
each one of us, alone, is worth nothing.
   Above all, always be capable of feeling
deeply any injustice committed against anyone,
anywhere in the world. This is the most
beautiful quality in a revolutionary.
   Until forever, my children. I still hope
to see you.
   A great big kiss and a big hug from,
   Papa

**Che Guevara in a letter to his children in 1965,
to be opened upon the event of his death**

Desiderata

Go placidly amid the noise and haste, and remember what peace there may be in silence.

As far as possible without surrender be on good terms with all persons.

*Speak your truth quietly and clearly; and listen to others, even the dull and ignorant;
they too have their story.*

*Avoid loud and aggressive persons, they are vexatious to the spirit.
If you compare yourself with others, you may become vain and bitter;
for always there will be greater and lesser persons than yourself.*

*Enjoy your achievements as well as your plans. Keep interested in your career,
however humble; it is a real possession in the changing fortunes of time.*

Exercise caution in your business affairs, for the world is full of trickery.

*But let this not blind you to what virtue there is; many persons strive for high ideals;
and everywhere life is full of heroism.*

*Be yourself. Especially, do not feign affection. Neither be critical about love; for in the
face of all aridity and disenchantment it is as perennial as the grass.*

Take kindly the counsel of the years, gracefully surrendering the things of youth.

*Nurture strength of spirit to shield you in sudden misfortune. But do not distress
yourself with imaginings. Many fears are born of fatigue and loneliness.*

Beyond a wholesome discipline, be gentle with yourself.

*You are a child of the universe, no less than the trees and the stars;
you have a right to be here.*

And whether or not it is clear to you, no doubt the universe is unfolding as it should.

*Therefore be at peace with God, whatever you conceive Him to be, and whatever
your labours and aspirations, in the noisy confusion of life keep peace with your soul.*

*With all its sham, drudgery and broken dreams, it is still a beautiful world.
Be cheerful. Strive to be happy.*

Max Ehrmann

Dear Emma,
    You will never lose by giving.

                    Love, Dad

A napkin note from Garth Callaghan, to his daughter, Emma

Life is meant to be fun, and joyous, and
fulfilling. May each of yours be that — having
each of you as a child of mine has certainly
been one of the good things in my life. Know
that I've always loved each of you with an
eternal, bottomless love.
   A love that has nothing to do with each
other, for I feel my love for each of you is
total and all-encompassing. Please watch out
for each other and love and forgive everybody.
It's a good life, enjoy it.

**Jim Henson in a letter to his children in 1986,
to be opened upon the event of his death**

Felicity Letcher

45, company director, Auckland, New Zealand

I have a really close relationship with my father, Philip Wallace Letcher; it's very loving. I'm the oldest of three daughters and all three of us have very different relationships with Phil. We get different things out of those relationships with him. For me, he has been a great mentor, someone I can confide in when worried. He talks to me whenever I get stuck, especially in business. And he's inspired great confidence in me. That means a lot.

He really believed in educating us. He said, 'That's my gift; the rest is up to you.' And it's a gift I've been able to use, that's enabled me to stand on my own two feet. Anything any of us wanted to do, he'd say, 'Yes, do that.' He told us to be passionate about what we want to do. And not to think about the money — just go out in the world and be passionate. I think that's quite brave.

My dad had a very tricky relation-ship with his own father. His father was a child of the Depression and a very good writer. He should have been a journalist or writer, but instead he got a job at the power board because he needed to bring money in. My dad set out to not be like that. I don't think he understood his father — he found him frustrating and they were really different people. Dad was the black sheep of the family, the creative one. He initially wanted to be a farmer. He sailed from a very early age, and earned enough money collecting empty bottles to build his first boat. He crewed on match-racing boats. He went to the world champs in Poland in the late sixties.

He left school at fourteen and worked as a butcher after trying farming. He started his own business at the age of eighteen. He was always selling something; always starting stuff up and watching it develop. He's never bought anything 'on tick'. He believes you earn the money and then you spend it. That's taught us a work ethic. Some of my fondest memories are of sitting and working with him out in the garage in our backyard after school, hearing the gossip, who was buying what, and learning business lessons like always leaving enough for the next person in the chain.

My mother is the backbone of my father. She's the anchor under the water and he's the boat that bobs around on top. Thanks to them, I set really firm boundaries and have high expectations for my two children, and I let them know it. I teach my children about finding something to be passionate about — like Dad taught me — and not to be scared to be different.

My son is very like my dad. He does a lot of the same peculiar things, like he likes to wear particular types of cotton and doesn't wear normal pyjamas. He's got a mind like my father. That's part of the DNA that's been carried on. He even kisses like Dad. Max likes it when I say, 'You are just like your poppa,' because he thinks Poppa is funny.

Dad had a brain tumour when I was overseas in 1994. They discovered it in his pituitary gland. He was getting headaches and it was a tumour pressing on his optic nerves. That changed him quite a

He really believed in educating us. He said, 'That's my gift; the rest is up to you.'

lot; it defined the second stage of my father. After the operation he became much more emotional. He couldn't control, for the first time in his life, what was happening to him. He took a lot of medication and it really affected him. He went through periods of depression. He also discovered yoga. Until really recently, he did yoga two times a day, seven days a week.

Now, we're moving into the third stage — he's seventy-six and he has been diagnosed with early onset dementia. About five years ago, we noticed he was starting to change, becoming less able to run his business effectively. He let it wind down until there wasn't anything left to sell. They sold the family home last year and now live in a little townhouse. It's much easier for them. When they dismantled the house, he was heartsick. He just went upstairs and left us to do it all.

He's accepted the diagnosis. He's not fighting it. His life has got a bit smaller. We go over and just be with him. I give him lots of physical affection; stroke his hand. He's always loved classical music and singing, and listening to music now is a big thing for him. He loves going to concerts, theatre, even dance, and he'll hold your hand the whole way through and just be in the moment. It's quite remarkable how the child becomes the parent. For us to now look after him and Mum is, in a way, a gift. This is the compassion you show them, that you give back to them. It's a really

Things you'll never regret doing: visiting your grandmother, standing up to a bully, skydiving, living in Paris, falling madly in love.

Sam de Brito